Desktop Publishing Skills

A Primer for Typesetting with Computers and Laser Printers

Desktop Publishing Skills

A Primer for Typesetting with Computers and Laser Printers

James Felici
Ted Nace

Addison-Wesley Publishing Company

Reading, Massachusetts • Menlo Park, California • Don Mills, Ontario
Wokingham, England • Amsterdam • Sydney • Singapore • Tokyo
Madrid • Bogotá • Santiago • San Juan

Library of Congress Cataloging-in-Publication Data
Felici, James.
Desktop publishing skills.
    Bibliography: p.
    Includes index.
    1. Electronic publishing. 2. Computerized typesetting.
3. Printing, Practical—Laser use in. 4. Microcomputers
—Programming. 5. Self-publishing—Data processing.
I. Nace, Ted. II. Title.
Z286.E43F44 1987   070.5′028′5   86-26471
ISBN 0-201-11537-9

Reprinted with corrections August, 1987
Reproduced by Addison-Wesley from camera-ready copy supplied by the authors.

Many of the designations used by manufacturers and sellers to distinguish their products are claimed as trademarks. Where those designations appear in this book, and Addison-Wesley was aware of a trademark claim, the designations have been printed in initial caps or all caps.

    CDEFGHIJ-AL-898

Preface

In 1874, the Remington Company began marketing the first "desktop publishing" machine. Designed by the American inventor Christopher Sholes, this device—the typewriter—compressed the complex typesetting and printing process into a single step. The typewriter performed an inflexible, highly simplified form of typesetting: uniform, rigidly spaced characters in a single standardized typeface.

The advent of computerized word processing did not profoundly affect type quality—printers remained little more than computer-driven typewriters. However, laser printers—whose ability to place marks on paper is defined by software rather than hardware—have changed the office document forever and made typesetting accessible to millions of personal computer users. We've written this book to provide you with a solid grounding in the fundamentals of electronic publishing so you can take full advantage of the power that laser printers and desktop publishing technology offer you.

With laser printers you have complete power over the appearance of your documents. Indeed, laser printers and the typesetting power they offer have changed the standard of what office documents should look like. This makes publishing both an opportunity and a challenge—to control all aspects of how a publication will look. Whether you are a business person, student, professional, or traditional publisher, you are empowered by these technologies to personally take control over the publishing process. In this book, we prepare you for that challenge by exploring the fundamentals of traditional and electronic publishing—typography, typesetting, design, and systems integration—so that you can take full advantage of this technology today and as it evolves in years to come.

With our publishing backgrounds we fully appreciate the complexity of the publishing process and we recognize that no technology can make it a push-button proposition. For the foreseeable future, successful publishing—whether for in-house use or for commercial venture—will rely on traditional skills and knowledge. For this reason, we have taken a conservative approach in this book: we believe that you can do the best job when armed with a solid foundation of facts and fundamentals, not just advice and a smattering of how-to.

By and large, we've focused not on today's products, which are transitory and rapidly changing, but on the fundamental principles of typography, typesetting, design, graphics, and the personal computer systems that will work for you. These are the things you will need to know in order to make good equipment buying decisions and to get the most of that equipment. We offer the professional expertise that you need in order to create professional-looking documents, whether they're in the office, the marketplace, or just among friends.

The worlds of publishing and personal computers are steadily converging, and we fully expect them to continue drawing closer together, with each borrowing increasingly from the other. That point of convergence, too, has helped to define the scope of this book: while other sorts of computers have benefited from the desktop publishing revolution, our emphasis is on the popular personal computers that are its driving force: the Apple Macintosh and the IBM PC family and other MS-DOS machines.

It is our general thesis that tools work best in the hands of those who understand what they do and how to use them. The tools alone do not make the craftsman, yet desktop publishing presents you with several new toolboxes to work with. The watershed character of desktop publishing is illustrated in us as authors—a publishing professional and a computer journalist combining our knowledge to create a complete overview of this new, compressed world. In large part, this book was born out of the concerns and questions our publishing comrades had over the problems and opportunities offered by these new tools—each had a piece of the puzzle, but not a clear vision of the whole picture.

Desktop publishing requires you to wear many hats, from editor to typesetter to designer. Each task has its own toolbox, but more importantly, each demands its own set of skills and insights. With this book, we hope to make those hats fit comfortably and to give you the skills to choose your tools wisely and use them well.

San Francisco

J.F.
T.N.

Contents

THE ELEMENTS OF PUBLISHING

THE DESKTOP TOOLBOX

Chapter 1

In-House Publishing

Any revolution must be defined relative to the status quo, and the key to the desktop publishing revolution is the availability of the major publishing tools. In contrast to traditional publishing, in which the cost of equipment dictates that it can be owned only by the largest companies or by professional publishing services, the tools of desktop publishing—a microcomputer (or personal computer) and a desktop laser printer—are compact and inexpensive enough to be a practical purchase for almost any business.

The tools have become more compact, but the process remains largely unchanged—it's a complex system with many steps. The new system gives an unprecedented degree of control to an aspiring publisher, but it also places a burden on the individual who is now called upon to do the work of many. A major question, then, becomes, "What portions of the publishing process can feasibly be brought in-house, and will they really fit comfortably on one desktop?" The answer depends not just on the size of the desk, but how many hours you want to spend there and how many hats you want to wear—author, editor, designer, typographer, production artist, and printer.

Setting the Stakes: Rating Document Complexity

The concept of publishing is quite straightforward: it consists of taking an idea, elucidating it in words and/or pictures, and distributing the product in some physical form, usually on paper. It becomes more complex when you want to emphasize readability, and when you take into account the numbers in which the final version must be produced and how it will compete for attention when it's presented to its audience. The success of a publication will not ride on its content alone—the presentation can be vital to the fulfillment of its mission.

When looking at alternatives in the steps of the publishing process, both functional and aesthetic considerations must be taken into account. Often, one system can meet both the aesthetic and functional goals. Typesetting, for instance, is not only a fast and efficient way of generating text for reproduction, it also provides very pleasing aesthetic effects—the two factors have become tightly linked. The word processing system, on the other hand, is a more strictly functional system, mainly performing the necessary text manipulation tasks with few aesthetic refinements. Word-processed text is readable, but typeset presentation makes it more likely that the message will indeed be read.

The elements of the publishing industry have traditionally been described by their relative sophistication in the market spectrum, ranging from the low end to the high end. In any approach to publishing, it makes sense to first decide what kind of approach to take—how sophisticated your publication should be—and then be consistent about what part of this continuum you work in. It makes little sense, for instance, to use low-end typesetting, low-end graphic reproductions, low-end camera work, and high-tech printing. Likewise, it makes little sense to buy the finest fonts and typesetting equipment and then print your work at the local quick-print shop or on a xerox machine. The principle of the lowest common denominator is at work here: the quality of the whole will be limited by the lowest-quality element in the overall production equation.

Carried a step further, these same considerations apply to the economic aspects of publishing: the portion of the publishing effort that dominates as a budget item will define the economies of the other constituent parts. If printing is going to amount to 90 percent of a work's publishing budget, it won't make sense to skimp on the other 10 percent: the editorial, design, typesetting, and production costs. Understanding these relationships is the key to performing the cost analyses that you must do before embarking on building a desktop publishing system.

At the low end of the publishing spectrum is the office memo. Typically, it is typewritten, photocopied, and distributed by hand. The message is everything, and the format is determined by company standards. Of course, even the office memo is subject to technological enhancement, such as that available from a word processing system, which can hold boilerplate documents in memory, eliminate the need for retyping to add corrections, and output to a variety of printers with a variety of type styles. These are essentially functional improvements, though, as the office memo makes no great aesthetic demands. Presumably, the very nature of the message ensures that it will be read.

As readership of a given piece becomes more discretionary, though, presentation style becomes more important. The impact and effectiveness of a simple sales report is enhanced by eye-catching graphics and an engaging presentation. As we move up the market into the world of brochures and fliers, presentation can determine which publications will be picked off a table, and once they are picked up, which will present their messages most forcefully.

Bringing Production In-House

Once you've set the standards you'll aim for, you must decide what portions of the publishing system to bring in-house. This decision is difficult, and the choice must be made on the basis of several factors. The first is the increased control an in-house system can provide over the publishing effort (and the increased responsibilities that accompany control). Clearly, the more work you do in-house, the more direct control you have over it. Second is cost; is that control worth the extra expenditures involved? The third factor—one that is largely dependent on the first two—is the quality you're aiming for. The quality of the product is linked to the skills of the people creating it; even with very sophisticated tools, a trained hand is usually needed. Quality may be limited by the amount of money that can be spent to bring the necessary tools and expertise under one roof.

A microcomputer-based publishing system is appropriate for many situations, bringing together all three considerations—in-house control, low cost, and high quality. It doesn't offer the highest quality available, or the lowest cost, but given the new degree of control you have over the process, these compromises may be more than worthwhile. Even with the publishing hardware in-house, however, there are still many choices to be made about personnel and time investments.

Remember, too, that in most cases what is called desktop publishing really only affects "prepress" operations: editorial, typesetting, graphics, and page production. Two of the linchpins of the traditional publishing process are notably absent: printing and distribution.

If you are planning to publish in high volume, you'll probably need recourse to traditional methods for these two operations. Desktop laser printers are not designed to work as printing presses—they simply aren't built to handle high-volume, high-speed output. Nothing inherent in laser printing technology prevents laser printers from acting in this capacity—in fact, laser printers that can handle heavy output do exist, but at a price of 20 to 50 times the cost of their desktop cousins.

The following chapters will show what equipment and skills each step of the publishing process requires and how these processes can be carried on in-house—or what you should know about hiring outside services.

Chapter 2

The Publishing Process

Taking on new roles as a desktop publisher requires an understanding of what goes on throughout the publishing process—a respect for the many distinct yet interrelated jobs that go into the creation of a published work, and a proper observance of the cooperation—and boundaries—between these jobs necessary for the smooth operation of the system. This chapter outlines the traditional process and how the stages of that process have been affected by developments in the new desktop technologies.

In general, the publishing process is linear, proceeding step by step, and in the traditional arrangement there are few stages that go on simultaneously. The efforts and successes of one stage rely on the success of what has gone before. This intimate linkage is often invisible to one member of the production chain whose vision is obscured by the demands of one small bailiwick. Those farther downstream in the process are most acutely aware of their dependence on those carrying out earlier stages.

At the head of the stream is the author, who mills out the original manuscript. Next in line are the editor and copy editor, who polish the manuscript into its final form. From there the manuscript is borne to the designer, whose job it is to match the verbal conceptions of the author with a complementary visual presentation. In addition to designing the look of the pages and how illustrations and graphic elements will be handled, the designer also makes the typographic decisions that determine how the text of the publication will look. The manuscript, marked with all of its type specifications, is next sent to the typographer, who creates a high-quality typeset master image of the text, from which the final printed pages will be reproduced. While the type is being set, the final touches are being put on all the photographs and illustrations that will accompany the text. When typeset text and illustrations are assembled, the whole package is given to a graphic artist who, working under the guidelines developed by the designer, "pastes up" the various text and art elements in their relative positions on each page. A stripper then photographically transforms the pages into film negatives, and these negatives are sent to the printer who uses them to create the printing plates that actually carry the ink onto the paper. Once the printing is complete, the pages are folded, trimmed, and bound—sometimes by the printer, sometimes by yet another specialist, the binder.

The divisions of labor associated with these steps are not always so neatly drawn, especially as electronic publishing technologies mature and some of these once distinct phases melt into single operations. Probably the most prevalent shortcut is the merging of text and graphics on one typeset page, obviating the pasteup production process. Indeed it is just this ability to trim steps that has generated much of the excitement over the emergence of desktop publishing tools.

Editorial

Since the microcomputer and word processing software have become such popular workplace tools, editorial is probably the most familiar phase of the publishing process. Editorial is the phase in which the manuscript is prepared, and it is ultimately the reason why the rest of the publishing system exists at all. Ironically, it is also usually one of the most underbudgeted steps in the whole process.

The editorial process can be divided into two phases: manuscript assembly and editing. This can involve just one person doing all the writing and editing alone. At the other extreme is database publishing, like that involved in publishing an encyclopedia, in which hundreds of data input workers feed information to scores of editors who collect, organize, and verify the information.

The mechanics of the editorial process aside, its purpose is the creation of polished text of a quality that does justice to the time, effort, and money spent publishing it. Even at the lowest end of the spectrum the message should be clear, concise, and worth saying. That most people are familiar and at ease with this portion of the publishing process should not cloud the fact that there is always a higher standard of editorial quality to aspire to, and clarity of communication usually results in very tangible economies attributable to the effectiveness of the final publication.

Typically, the cost of editorial excellence is quite low in relation to the overall publishing cost equation. An editor (or the lack of one) can often make or break a publication, be it a book, magazine, sales report, or marketing flier. In the computer industry, for instance, fortunes have been made and lost in large part based on the clarity, completeness, and style of the products' technical documentation.

Even the most cheaply produced publication can be effective if its editorial content is strong. Likewise, huge production costs cannot salvage an unintelligible manuscript.

Easing the editorial burden for the desktop publisher is a new generation of editorial software appearing for the microcomputer. Spelling checkers are now widely used, and developments in computer artificial intelligence have spawned programs that can detect many common grammar and usage problems, such as verb/noun number disagreements, incorrect use of homonyms (such as there and their), sentence fragments, and incorrect punctuation. As useful as these tools are, however, they are no substitute for a competent human editor. The spelling checkers with the largest dictionaries cannot correct *the* where *them* is needed, and the most advanced logic tools can't point out a missing description or a redundant paragraph.

Design

Advertising is perhaps the most obvious example of the use of design in publications. In ads, design often predominates over the verbal message, but in any publication design is key. For most readers, the design aspects of a publication are largely invisible, but their impact on how we perceive a publication, how effective its message is, and, to a great extent, its credibility, hinge on both obvious and subtle design considerations. The eye is caught by the splashier elements of design—photos, graphics, colors, headlines—but the mind is often hooked by more low-key elements. Never underestimate the impact of typefaces that project an image of authority, jazziness, scholarliness, or calm; page layouts that are reminiscent of nostalgic scenes; designs with an open, airy presentation or a dense, urgent look; or a page design that projects order and structure or informality and lightheartedness.

All of these elements are part of a visual vocabulary that most people respond to intuitively but which they are not very adept at expressing. This is largely due to the fact that schools do not emphasize organized training in the visual arts, and few have had the opportunities or the tools to express themselves visually instead of verbally—until now, that is, when microcomputers have made the tools of graphic communication widely available.

Putting these tools in the hands of inexperienced users will undoubtedly result initially in a deluge of unsophisticated and downright ugly publications. But in the long run, these tools may bring some of the fundamental principles of the visual arts home in a way that art classes in school never did.

The first phase of publication design is the overall conceptual design of the work. This includes decisions on such factors as page size, use of color, text arrangement on the page, methods of incorporating graphics and photographs, selection of typefaces, the use of color, text formatting style, and the use of decorative rules, borders, or graphic elements. The finished look of any professionally designed page is the result of dozens of small design decisions.

Every document has a design, although many publications are designed by default; that is, their look derives from a lack of design decisions. Take, for instance, a business letter—apart from the design of the corporate logotype, there is little time spent designing its layout. The text blocks are arranged mostly by convention, and about the only design prerogative that is exercised over it is how the words are placed on the page: they can be typed or output on an office printer in either monospacing or proportional spacing. The printer may offer some control over the typeface. In terms of design, this is a low-end document, and one of its major design considerations is its uniformity of appearance relative to other issuances of its kind.

With the introduction of graphics and typeset text, documents take a major leap forward in design complexity, but still cover a broad range. The repertoire of design devices for a page bearing only type, for instance, is quite limited; most unillustrated book pages (like those of most novels) tend to look pretty much the same. The only real variables the designer has to work with on such a page are typeface, type size, graphic elements such as boxes and rules, and the placement of the type on the page. Because an all-type page runs the risk of appearing dense, gray, and formidable, these few devices are used to "open up" the layout. The key becomes the manipulation of white space—a dense, gray layout discourages the reader from venturing into the page.

The addition of illustrations to a page allows the designer to break free of the boxy format imposed by the all-text page. The challenge of successfully illustrating a document is to add what are usually rectangular graphics in a way that does not merely reinforce a blocky layout. On the other hand, illustrations must be restrained from becoming mere decorative elements that can give a page a cluttered, distracting look.

The key to the importance of design considerations is the audience for the publication. A publication meant to sway potential clients needs more attention to design than a club newsletter. The medium is, if not the whole message, an integral part of how the message will be accepted. Even a sales pitch must dress for success.

It is at this design level that most publications must be approached, and the importance of good design cannot be underestimated. No matter how good the message is on its pages, an unattractive document is less likely to be read and less likely to be taken seriously. The design reflects upon the publisher and the product. Commercial publishers are acutely aware of this, and successful graphic designers can be very well paid. The payoff for the publisher comes when a consumer reaches for one magazine or book instead of another at a newsstand or bookstore. And in the office environment, the attractive report will leap out in contrast to the tedious gray mountain of word-processed documents and gaudily adorned issuances of novice desktop publishers. Good design catches the eye and invites the reader inside.

Designers stand to benefit greatly from desktop publishing technologies, especially the development of so-called *WYSIWYG* (what-you-see-is-what-you-get) systems. WYSIWYG systems allow the designer to preview on the computer's screen the pages as they will appear in their printed form. They can try out a wide variety of page and type designs very quickly without having to paste up mock-ups of every prospective design. For the beginning designer, the electronic approach allows for extensive experimentation to better explore the design process.

Typesetting

Familiar word processing systems offer a primitive form of typesetting. There are two main differences between word processing and true typesetting, however: the degree of text formatting capability and the quality of the printed output.

Word processing programs can be viewed as subsets of commercial typesetting systems. Both rely on assigning typographic attributes to selected passages of text, typically by inserting formatting codes into the text. In some systems these codes are visible on the computer screen, but others (including WYSIWYG systems) instead display the results of those commands on the screen.

A third group relies on generic labels or tags that are inserted into the text. These generic labels (such as *Headline, Caption, Main Text, Footnote*) are then translated by the computer into the appropriate formatting commands, which have been defined in specification tables, or *style sheets*. These approaches are examined in detail in Chapter 6.

An important difference between typesetting and word processing formatting capabilities is the control typesetting gives over space: space between words, between letters, and between lines. The sophistication of the typographer's text-formatting language allows for the creation of finished text that is exceptionally good-looking and readable. Although typesetting systems are beginning to become easier to use, this degree of sophistication has traditionally demanded a very skillful and experienced keyboarder, working for wages generally considerably higher than that of a word processing operator.

The formatting sophistication of commercial typesetting systems is complemented by the high aesthetic quality of the type they create. Today's digital type-setting machines—of which the desktop laser printer is a low-end example—create images built from tiny dots. Commercial phototypesetters expose the character images onto photosensitive paper by means of direct laser impact or images generated on a very fine-resolution cathode ray tube (CRT). Commercial-quality digital type starts at resolutions of about 600 dots per inch (dpi) and goes to more than 5000 dpi.

The use of photographic paper is an important element in the fine quality of commercially set type. Evenly distributed, minute particles of silver in the paper give great control over the exposure of the paper, allowing little spillover of light that could create fuzzy images.

The use of this silver-rich photosensitive paper has several ramifications. One is that the cost of the silver as well as the cost of the chemicals and equipment needed to develop the paper adds considerably to the cost of typesetting. It also means that the typeset output cannot be used as a final product because a page can only be exposed on one side, it discolors over time, it scratches easily, and it is generally too expensive to use, especially for multiples of the same document.

In many respects, desktop laser printers are the functional equivalents of commercial typesetting machines. The typefaces they generate are created by computer software, so there is no physical limitation on the number of different typefaces they can print on one page or in the sizes at which those typefaces are printed. In this way, they are freed from the encumbrances of other printers like typewriters or daisy-wheel printers that rely on a mechanical impact device to print letters on a page.

The main differences between desktop laser printers and phototypesetting machines are that they have lower print resolution (typically 300 dpi) and they print on plain paper, like an office photocopier. The laser printer works by creating the image of a page first on a photosensitive rotating drum which attracts minute particles of toner (a kind of dry ink) in the shapes of the letters. The image thus created on the drum is offset onto the paper and fused in place by heat. (More about the mechanics of laser printing is included in Chapter 9.)

It is its similarities to typesetting that have given laser printing the moniker "desktop publishing." The laser printer's ability to emulate higher resolution type-setters have even made it popular in the world of commercial typography as a proofing device. Although laser printing's resolution is too low to meet commercial standards, the similarities of output of the two technologies make it possible to preview typeset matter without using expensive silver-based photographic paper.

The typesetting phase starts after the editors have finished their work on the manuscript and the designer has created a complete set of typographic specifications. It's now up to the typographer to carry out the designer's instructions. Executing these instructions can be extremely complex. In a financial table from a company's annual report, for example, the number of keystrokes needed to format the text can outnumber the text keystrokes by more than 5 to 1.

Before microcomputers arrived on the scene, manuscripts were typically delivered to the typographer in typewritten form, and a keyboarder would then rekey the text into the typesetting system. Considering the labor and overhead costs of the typical type shop, this is very expensive typing. Now that clients usually create and store their documents on word processors, manuscripts can be delivered to the typesetter in an electronic form that the type shop can use or translate with its own equipment, avoiding costly rekeying.

The most straightforward delivery method is sending a floppy disk to the type shop. Another alternative is delivering the manuscript over the phone lines, using a modem. Some systems allow remote microcomputer users to use a modem to get directly on line with the typesetting computer—using the microcomputer to emulate one of the typesetting system's input terminals. This option allows the desktop publisher access to a commercial typesetting system that would otherwise be unaffordable. This process, called *interfacing*, is a very useful option if a job calls for the highest quality commercial type. Some systems allow a microcomputer to run the commercial software remotely and output proofs on a desktop laser printer. Then, after all corrections have been made, the document can be sent through the phototypesetter.

Most type shops employ proofreaders, whose job it is to verify the success of the coding efforts and to check for keyboarding input errors. One of the things clients pay for when they have their type set commercially is the guarantee of accuracy that comes with every job—if the typographer makes a mistake and the proofreader misses it, the type shop will generally make corrections for free. This puts a lot of pressure on the proofreader, and a quality proofreader is an invaluable cog in the publishing machinery, because the final reader—the audience—rightly perceives typos as a sign of sloppy work, and a reflection on the publisher.

Graphics

The illustrations that accompany text serve a dual function: they expand and elaborate upon the matter discussed in the text and they make the page more visually appealing. Generally, graphics can be created while the manuscript is still being edited. Their final size, though, cannot be firmly fixed until the manuscript goes to the page design stage.

Graphics may be divided into two categories: *halftones* (or *screened art*) and *line art*. These forms are distinguished by the processes that create them. Printing presses can print only solid colors; that is, they either lay down ink or leave an area of the paper blank. In order to produce midtones (for instance, the levels of gray in a black-and-white photo), images must be screened—converted into a pattern of fine dots whose size and placement give the eye the impression of lighter shades.

For newspaper work—which uses the coarsest of commercial halftones—photographs and halftone art are typically screened at 50 to 65 screen dots per inch. Fine magazine work is normally 120 to 150 screen dots per inch (see Chapter 11 for a detailed explanation of the difference between screen dots and typesetter dots). How finely a graphic should be screened depends largely on the printing technology used, as many lower-end printing presses and processes can deal only with more coarsely screened artwork.

Line art does not need to be screened, as it is composed solely of one consistently dense color tone. If all areas of a picture can be rendered in one color tone (all solid black, for instance, with no grays) it can be produced as line art. Line art reproduces better than screened art when you're using low-end printing systems. You can demonstrate this yourself by reproducing a glossy photograph on a photocopying machine. The photocopier can only reproduce blacks, and when grays become too light, the machine fails to pick them up. Line art may also be less expensive than screened art, because the screening process adds an extra step to production, while some line art can be incorporated into the pasted-up page in its original form.

In the past, all line art had to be generated by artists using traditional materials like pen and ink. Other nonphotographic illustrations had to be created in the same way. Today, however, graphic artists have the option of creating graphics on the computer, and like the designer, they can benefit from the computer's power to rapidly generate and alter images and designs. For many applications, using a computer can produce results equivalent to the traditional methods, and as computer graphics continue to improve, greater inroads will be made by computer-generated graphics.

The graphic capabilities at the high end of the computer market are far more sophisticated than those of microcomputers, but they come at the cost of very large capital outlays for hardware and have the disadvantage of technical demands that exclude most graphic artists. At the low end, where microcomputer programs currently reside, the computer environment is more accessible to the graphic artist, but the limitations it imposes on quality and results often prove frustrating. The tools alone do not make the craftsperson; it is important to have a graphic artist create the artwork if you need quality graphics.

Pasteup

After editorial and graphics are prepared, the next step is the process of assembling the master pages from which the final pages will be duplicated—commonly known as pasteup. Virtually all reproduction (printing) processes rely on having a master image from which duplicates are rendered. The exception to this, of course, is desktop laser printing, which is capable of creating finished pages from electronic data. But laser printers are generally incapable of creating large press runs of any lengthy document—it's simply not designed as a bulk printing press—so even if you output an original on a laser printer, you'll probably need to paste up *boards* (or *mechanicals*) of each page to be reproduced.

The pasteup artist assembles all of the materials needed to complete the page: text, photographs, graphics, and any other design elements being used, such as rules, background shading, or decorative borders. These elements are affixed to a piece of thick paper or cardboard in precise alignment. The pasteup boards are usually preprinted with a network of grid lines that provide the artist with alignment guides. These grid lines are printed in a pale blue, called *non-reproducing blue* because it does not show up when the board is photographed.

Each mechanical page must be equipped with *registration marks*, very finely drawn marks that lie outside of the area that will be printed. These marks are used to align—register—the pages when they are photographed and printed. This ensures that the page image will be printed in the proper—and uniform—position on each page.

Certain graphics cannot be effectively reproduced in a form that can be pasted on these boards. Finely screened photographs, for example, suffer losses in quality through the many stages of their creation, from original, to film negative, to paper positive (for pasteup), then back to film when the board is photographed prior to printing. To cut out some of these steps, the pasteup artist leaves a blank window in the page. A negative of the screened photograph will be affixed over that window at a later stage in a process called *stripping*.

Likewise, color elements cannot be pasted directly on the page. Because each color will have to be printed separately on the printing press, the pasteup artist creates several versions of a color-bearing page, each representing the printing area of a distinct color. Typically, a multicolor page demands the three primary colors (from which a whole rainbow of colors can be created) plus black. This is referred to as *four-color process*. When only one color is used along with the black, the process is called *duotone*. Duotone is far more economical than four-color work, and it is surprisingly effective in adding spark to a graphic presentation.

Another step in the creation of color graphics is *color separation*, an electromechanical process in which an original multicolor work is broken down into three or more distinct film negatives, each representing one color. Original graphic works may be created with these colors in mind, but to reproduce already finished color work or color photographs will demand color separation, which is fairly expensive.

Only when all of the page elements are in place and properly registered is the page said to be *camera-ready*. In order to create the final printing plates, the printer needs to be given camera-ready copy.

The pasteup process has been profoundly affected by desktop publishing technology, especially by page makeup software. These programs combine typesetting and pasteup into one procedure. They perform the same tasks as the hand process, but all of the text and art elements are manipulated in electronic form, which can speed up the process greatly, especially if last-minute design changes call for some pages to be entirely remade.

Page makeup—or pagination—software comes in two basic forms: *interactive* and *batch*. With an interactive program, pages are created one at a time—a process suitable for complex pages or where the treatment and placement of text and graphics varies greatly from page to page, as in much magazine work.

Batch programs, on the other hand, are ideal for documents whose page layouts are fairly standard, with little variation in how text and graphics are handled. In a batch-oriented system, general specifications for all of the pages are set out in advance. These include the number of lines of text on each page, how graphics and captions should be positioned, and where illustrations and footnotes should be positioned relative to their references in the main text. When all of the parameters have been established, the program paginates the document automatically, deciding where page breaks should occur and where all text and graphic elements are placed on each page. The automatic pagination of batch-oriented programs can save a vast amount of time and trouble in the layout of long documents, such as technical documentation, directories, and lightly illustrated textbooks.

In a desktop publishing system, this electronic pasteup may be the last stage of the publishing process. If all of the art elements can be incorporated by the pagination program and only a modest number of printed copies are needed, the laser printer can act as the printing press. If you need more copies than the laser printer can handle, the electronically pasted-up pages can be output from a laser printer or phototypesetter and used as camera-ready copy for the next steps of the printing process.

Film Stripping

For reproduction on a printing press, pages need to be converted into photographic film. After pasteup has been completed—either manual or electronic—the finished pages and any unincorporated artwork (usually screened photographs or color separations) go to a film stripper, who may or may not work for the printing company.

The film stripper creates photographic negatives of entire pages, stripping in film halftones and precisely registering all overlays for color work. An important step in the process is *opaquing*, during which the stripper inspects all of the film for flaws (usually tiny specks, dots, or shadows cast by pasted elements on the mechanical). If these flaws appear in a nonprinting area, the stripper will color them in—opaque them—with a special fluid or pencil. If the flaws appear in a printing area, the stripper may be able to scrape away the photographic emulsion causing the flaw.

From these film negatives, the film stripper produces *blueline* proofing copies, which the client can review as a last proofing step before printing. Making changes at this stage in the process is costly because it means restripping the page, but it's the last chance to make any corrections before you invest the high costs of printing. Bluelines, incidentally, like a builder's blueprints, get their name from the inexpensive process used to create them, which produces a blue image on a white background.

Electronic publishing techniques will soon change the role of the film stripper. Theoretically, once completed pages have been electronically pasted up, they can be imaged directly onto printing plates, bypassing the film-stripping stage. Fortunately for the film stripper, the cost of transferring page images directly from computer to printing plate is still prohibitive for most publishers. Furthermore, the extra quality control that the hand process offers makes it additionally appealing.

Printing

In all but the lowest volume print runs, printing will probably be the largest single item in the budget. It is the only step in the publishing process that is materials-intensive, and the predominant material is paper. While most offices are used to dealing with paper by the ream, printers routinely order their paper by the ton.

Paper is a sheet of interconnected cellulose fibers derived from plants—the longer the fibers, the more interconnected they can be, and, hence, the stronger the paper. The longest fibers (and the best for papermaking) are cotton and flax fibers, but they are expensive and are generally reserved for fine bond papers and artists' papers. Most of the paper we use daily is made from far less expensive wood pulp, which, because its fibers are much shorter than cotton's, is often supplemented with a number of additives to enhance its strength, appearance, and how it carries inks. The most common of these are bleach (for whiteness), starches (for strength and to control absorbency), fillers (to add bulk and increase opacity), and coatings (to create a variety of printing surfaces and absorbency characteristics).

Paper is an essential element in the printing equation, because it determines in large part the quality of the printing job. In color work, for instance, a coated paper is usually used so that the inks will sit on the surface of the page and not be absorbed down into the sheet. Such an effect adds brilliance to the final image.

Shopping for paper is often a matter of balancing desired results with affordability. Paper is usually the biggest item in the printing bill, and the larger the press run, the greater the cost will be.

After the paper cost, much of the remaining expense of printing goes for *make-ready,* the process of having the printing plates made, mounted on the press, and properly registered for accurate printing. The press is then run slowly to verify the accuracy of the adjustments and to check for overall print and color quality. Once the print quality is acceptable, the press is run up to normal speed, at which tens of thousands of copies may be run off per hour. Except for very simple, one-color jobs and very large press runs, make-ready hours routinely outnumber the hours actually spent printing, and the more complex or demanding the job, the more make-ready time is needed.

Still common are the processes of *relief printing* (in which ink is borne onto the paper via raised printing surfaces, as in "hot metal" type) and *gravure printing* (in which ink is carried in incised areas of a printing plate into which the paper is pressed to pick up the ink), but most printing work these days is done using *offset lithography,* the steps of which are fairly representative of all printing processes.

The first step in any printing process is the creation of the matrix that will carry the ink onto the paper. In the case of offset lithography, the vehicle is usually a flexible aluminum plate (although sometimes other materials are used, including cardboard for short runs). These plates are treated on one side with a photographic chemical coating. The film negatives created by the film stripper are laid over these plates in precise registration, and the plates are exposed to very bright light. After developing, the areas of the plate that were exposed to light will have a property that repels water but allows the oily printing ink to adhere. On the press, the plate is mounted on a roller that is constantly being wetted and inked; and because the ink and the water don't mix, the ink stays only on the printing areas of the plate, from which it is offset onto a rubber roller and then onto the paper.

Printing presses are of two types: *sheet-fed presses* and *web presses.* As the name implies, a sheet-fed press prints one precut sheet at a time. A web press, on the other hand, prints on a continuous ribbon of paper from a large roll. This ribbon, or web, is printed with several page impressions across its width, and at the end of the press the web is folded and cut into booklet-like configurations called *signatures.* Newspaper presses create the biggest of these—typically up to 64 pages—all created on one enormous sheet that is folded eight times, then trimmed at three edges. Magazines are printed the same way, although generally the signatures are smaller (8, 12, 16, 24, or 32 pages). These signatures are then bound en masse into their familiar shape. By looking at the edge of the binding, you can see how the signatures have been assembled. (This is particularly easy to see on a hardbound book.)

In general, the web press is reserved for large-run publications. Its large paper size and its design for high-speed operation make it uneconomical for small runs. Considering that web presses can print tens of thousands of impressions per hour, there's little point in setting one up for a small run; by the time the press gets up to running speed, the job is over. For these smaller jobs, or for jobs which need very exacting color work (which can require slower operating speeds) a sheet-fed press is usually employed.

One of the reasons that traditional printing technology can create such high-quality results is that the system is based on a dedicated printing matrix; that is, each printing plate is created specifically for the job at hand. By comparison, laser printers and xerographic machines may be said to use an "erasable" matrix (the toner drum), and the flexibility demanded by an erasable matrix limits the precision and quality of its printing results. In addition, traditional printing technologies use inks whose characteristics (thickness, drying time, tackiness, and so on) are variable and whose application to the paper can be rigidly controlled. Finally, the printer has the option to use one of a wide variety of paper types, many of which are not compatible with desktop laser printers.

Binding

One of the thorniest dilemmas for the desktop publisher is deciding how to bind together the printed pages. Traditional in-house methods that can be performed by hand include ring binding (looseleaf notebook style) and clip-on binding (report covers). At a more sophisticated level are a number of binding options based on light equipment that can be brought in-house without necessitating extensive training or mechanical expertise. Such systems include plastic *tubular binding* (in which the edges of the pages are perforated with a series of rectangular holes that are engaged by the fingers of the plastic binding), *post binding* (in which the pages are drilled as for looseleaf binding and the pages are bolted together), and *side stitching* (in which the pages are stapled along one edge). In addition to these traditional binding forms, there are also a number of patented binding systems available that use such devices as a plastic spine with widely spaced tines that link the pages through a series of drilled holes. Some of these systems can bind volumes up to several inches thick, accommodating a wide variety of paper thicknesses.

An inexpensive and durable (but more mechanically complex) binding method is *saddle stitching*, in which the binding is formed at a fold through which staples are driven; this is a common binding for magazines. Certain publications, though, require a more booklike binding treatment, the most common of which is called *perfect binding*. If you've ever had a paperback book fall to pieces in you lap, you may be willing to argue that "perfect" is a misnomer, but when executed properly with a good stock of paper, perfect binding can be very durable. Perfect binding is based on the assembly of single sheets or signatures whose folded edges are scored, coated thickly with glue, and then wrapped with a cover. When the glue sets, it holds the signatures to each other and all of the pages to the cover.

There are, of course, many publications that may not need to be bound, and for these documents a simple pattern of folds may suffice. When creating a folded piece, however, you must make sure that the printing method and the paper used are compatible with folding. Many kinds of ink and paper will not tolerate folding without cracking.

The Right Tools for the Job

The possession of a microcomputer and a laser printer puts into your hands the tools of the typographer, but, as should be clear from the preceding discussion, there's much more to publishing than typesetting. Even at its simplest, laser-printed output is clearly superior to that produced by any other currently and widely available desktop printing method. With such a desktop system, you have the ability to create truly professional-looking output at unprecedentedly low costs. To achieve that quality, however, you'll need to consider several issues, from design to paper quality.

The traditional publisher hires many experts to take on these responsibilities. Determining how many of these publishing tasks you want to take on and how many you'll want to hire out depends on your publication, your staff, and your budget. Like the traditional publisher, the desktop publisher has to learn about the entire publishing process in order to make informed decisions about the highly interdependent steps that go into getting a work into print.

Fortunately, the desktop publishing environment is scaled down in almost all respects from its traditional commercial counterpart, so mastery of these elements is feasible. A serious mistake among publishing novices, though, is to underestimate the breadth of the undertaking. In the ensuing chapters we will be introducing the concepts and processes of both commercial publishing and its desktop counterpart, providing a perspective on how the latter emulates—and diverges from—the former and the best methods to use for your task.

Chapter 3

Looking at "Typeset Quality"

Until the development of the laser printer there was a wide gulf between the low end (word processing) and the high end (phototypesetting) of the text-processing realm. The limited computing ability of the early generations of microcomputers and—more importantly—the typographic limitations imposed by office impact printers combined to put a ceiling on what word processing programs could do or even needed to do. Those who wanted professional-looking publications invested in professional publishing services.

The desktop laser printer has provided a middle ground between these two extremes—it acts like a typesetting machine, but it's priced like a good impact printer. Just as word processing software is a junior version of typesetting programs, the desktop laser printer should be seen as a junior version of the commercial typesetting machine. The laser printer shares many functions and abilities with the larger machines. In a laser printer, as in commercial digital typesetting, the characters and other marks to be printed are defined not by hardware (such as a daisy wheel) but by software. Any mark that can be defined by software—including versions of traditional commercial typefaces—can be generated by the laser printer. This has opened up a new world for the desktop printer.

The rallying cry of the pilgrims into this new land was "typeset quality," or for the less brazen, "near typeset quality." Certainly, the new type bears a closer resemblance to commercial type than that offered by the impact printer, but the boast begs the question: What exactly is typeset quality?

The key to the claim of "typeset quality" is the use of commercial-style typefaces—the carefully limned, proportionally spaced type designs that have been used by typographers for centuries. This is clearly a major breakthrough for the appearance of the printed office word, but even a quick comparison of the appearance of laser type and commercial type reveals that the quality of commercial type is based on more than the right typeface.

In the end, trying to define "typeset quality"—and in so doing to make it a meaningful standard—is a useless exercise. It is far better to understand the sources of quality in typesetting and use that knowledge to judge the appropriate quality for jobs at hand. The best way to do this is to look into some of these sources of quality in commercial type.

Clarity and Resolution

Clarity is the crispness with which characters are defined on the page—the sharpness of each letter's image. It's an important element of the appearance and readability of a page and a function of several factors.

In the early days of phototypesetting, type was created on photographic paper by shining a bright light through a film negative that bore images of the full character set of a given typeface. The letters were exposed one at a time. For this method, clarity was a function of the size of the final projected image, as controlled by a series of lenses, in relation to the master image on the negative. If the image was enlarged too much, its focus softened and the crispness of the image suffered.

With the development of digital type, the images of letters were generally created on a CRT against which the photographic paper was pressed, and the image on the tube was exposed onto the film—no lenses, no focusing problem. In digital type, though, the characters are assembled from many dots or lines (a process called *raster imaging*), and unless these building blocks are very minute, they can be detected by the eye, especially on curved edges of the characters (see Figure 3-1). This jagged-edge problem becomes more apparent in larger type sizes.

For this reason it is common to hear the term *resolution* used in relation to issues of type clarity. The higher the resolution—typically expressed as dots (or lines) per inch—the clearer the image and the smoother the outline. Most desktop laser printers print 300 dots per inch, and at this resolution the characters are actually less clear than those created by a decent daisy-wheel printer. The design of the characters, however, is so superior to impact printer type that the the overall effect is one of enhanced legibility.

In digital type, clarity is a matter of more than just dots per inch—it depends also on how the imaging technique uses those dots. Commercial typesetting machines use photographic paper as a substrate for producing type. The images of the characters are cast directly onto the film in the form of precisely controlled arrays of light. This creates images that are completely faithful to the "drawings" created by the software and projected by the high-resolution CRT's or extremely fine laser beams. It also creates high typesetting bills, because the silver-based film is quite

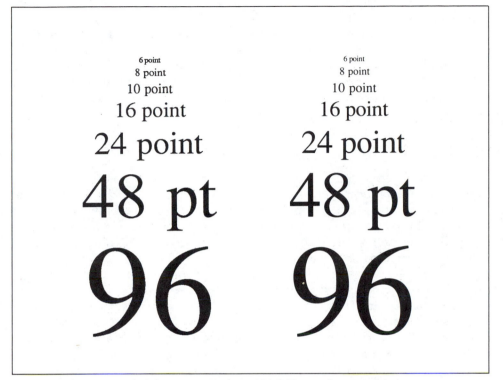

Figure 3-1 *The type on the left was generated on a 300 dpi laser printer on plain paper; the type on the right is from a 1270 dpi commercial typesetter using silver-based photographic paper. In the laser-printed sample, the low resolution makes the small type look somewhat muddy, and although the larger type appears more clean, the coarse dot structure is clearly visible, especially along the edges of the diagonal lines in the 96-point sample.*

expensive—for what you would pay for about five feet of this film you could buy a ream of paper for a laser printer.

Laser printers use a xerographic imaging process, in which the laser strikes a photosensitive drum, creating patterns of static electrical charges that attract particles of toner. The pattern of toner particles is then offset onto the paper and fused onto its surface with heat. Several generations of reproduction are involved in the process, and at each stage some loss of quality is inevitable. First the image is drawn onto the drum (generation one); then toner particles adhere to the charged patterns stenciled by the laser (generation two); then the toner is melted onto the paper, whose surface texture will affect the look of the final transferred image (generation three). The long and the short of this is that a silver-film-based system will create clearer type than a plain paper system.

One of the fundamental elements in the commercial-type quality equation, then, is the silver photo paper and the superior clarity it allows. Special papers are being developed specifically for laser printers, and refinements to the xerographic process will further enhance their performance. But for the present, the same technologies that make laser printing so affordable put a ceiling on the clarity of the image.

Spacing Control

A second major yardstick for measuring quality in typesetting is a function more of software than of hardware—the precision with which characters are placed on the page. In typography this is generally referred to as *white space control*, and one of the most important features for a typesetting system to have is sophisticated handling of such control. White space control is not just an aesthetic consideration; it is strictly related to the primary function of the type: readability.

Typography and typeface design have strong mathematical underpinnings, but their basic elements and principles have been arrived at almost exclusively through visual means. The reading eye has proved to be the best measuring gauge and the most natural design tool. Over the centuries, refinements to typeface design and use have come through a long process of trial and error, a search for what elements create the most readable and best looking page.

A key to readability is the frequency of alternating light and dark created by the black strokes of the letterforms against the light background upon which they are printed. There is an ideal range of light-dark frequency that maximizes legibility—where the eye can most effortlessly discern the letters and the words that are built from them. It is the control of this frequency that is one of the fundamental sources of quality in type (see Figure 3-2).

It is simple to observe how much easier and more pleasant it is to read a typeset book than a typewritten document. The reason for this lies in the typeset text's superior light-dark rhythm, which enhances readability. Typewriter type and most impact printer type is handicapped by its monospacing—the letters are designed so that each one takes up an equal amount of horizontal space on the page. If all of our alphabet's letters were of equal width, this would present far less of a problem, but there are *l*'s and there are *m*'s. The mechanically simplest way to make a typewriter or printer, of course, is to ignore these differences and allow the printing element to move a fixed amount after each letter is typed—a motion called *escapement*.

Fixed escapement, though, forces awkward design characteristics on monospaced alphabets. In order to create some semblance of regularity in the character

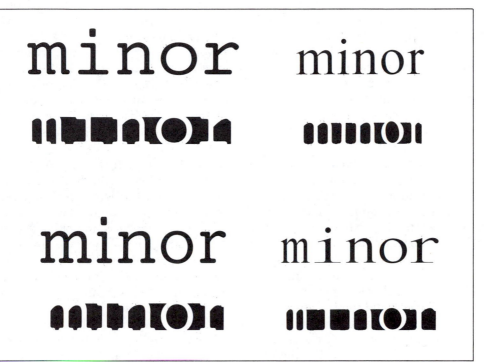

Figure 3-2 *Here, type samples have been paired with their reversed images to highlight the contrast between the character strokes and their background. In the upper left, Prestige Elite, a popular monospaced typewriter face, shows the irregular stroke frequency that makes it hard to read. By contrast, the Times Roman sample at upper right displays the even frequency that makes it so legible.*

At lower left, the monospaced Prestige Elite has been redesigned to be proportionally spaced. Note the more even rhythm of the vertical strokes. On the lower right, Times Roman has been converted into a monospaced font, dramatically illustrating the distortions necessary to create an alphabet whose characters all have the same width. (Courtesy Bigelow & Holmes)

set, the letters tend to be very wide and constructed of very thin strokes. The white background predominates over the dark letters, but some sense of consistent over-all color—an overall balance of light and dark across the page—is maintained. This wide set is mandated for tolerable levels of readability, but it seriously slows reading, and it means that monospaced type takes up a great deal of room horizontally on the page. In addition, because of the excessive amount of horizontal white space, additional vertical white space—in the form of extra line spacing—is needed to create a sense of visual balance. Tight line spacing looks quite natural in commercially typeset matter, but such tightness in a typewritten document creates the impression of a dense forest of marks covering the page.

The first efforts in the word processing world to reduce this problem resulted in proportional-spacing impact printers. These printers divide the letters of the alphabet into a small number of groups according to their widths. A typical proportional-spacing scheme may provide three units of escapement for every one on a monospaced machine. A wide character, like an *M*, would be accorded a width of three units, a narrower *e* would be accorded two, and an *i* would be measured as one unit wide.

Commercial typesetting systems also use the proportional approach, but they use many more units per character width. An industry standard at the moment is 54 units, but systems featuring 100-unit measuring schemes are becoming more and more common. This means that escapement can be tailored very closely to the width of specific characters. The result is that characters do not have to be designed around the constraints of the printer; rather, they can be designed for optimum legibility and beauty. Superior horizontal spacing also begets the potential for more natural line spacing. Because laser printers aren't limited by the mechanical restrictions of impact printer printheads, they can use this fine system of measurement, and they can use commercial-style typefaces.

This ability of software-generated characters to match up with custom-measured escapement may be a great leap in readability, but there is much more to the spacing issue. Consider first the varying shapes of letters and the shapes they present to letters that appear next to them. These shapes may be flat (*M*, *n*, *E*), round (*e*, *O*, *c*) or angular (*w*, *V*, *A*). Likewise, they may cordon off areas of white space on their flanks (*T*, *L*). A major typographic problem is how to get these shapes to fit against one another to avoid distracting gaps in the important frequency of alternating black and white.

The solution to this character-fitting problem is a process called *kerning*, in which minor adjustments are made to the white space between letters on a case-by-case basis. This may be done by creating a table of specific letter combinations and the spacing adjustments they need (*pair kerning*) or by creating a system that analyzes the shapes of adjoining characters and adjusts the space accordingly (*sector kerning*). No matter which way a system kerns, the typesetting computer must refer to these fitting guidelines for every two adjoining characters—an enormous and potentially time-consuming computing task. For this reason, extensive automatic kerning programs have typically been left out of microcomputer-based text processing programs (although their use is becoming more common).

Another important element in achieving well-spaced type is control over *tracking*, which is the overall tightness of letter spacing. Certain typefaces need to be more tightly letterspaced than others. In addition, large type—headline type,

B
ack in the late '60s, someone had the bright idea that everyone should use the same methods for marking up matter to be typeset. This would allow unfettered data interchange among people using different text processing systems and different nomenclature for identifying text elements. It would also enable authors to pre-code their manuscripts for publishers, facilitate a unified look among all of one organization's publications, and simplify printing-on-demand applications by allowing generic tags to be translated into the output code demanded by anybody's system.

Figure 3-3 *The typesetting term for the large initial capital in this figure is* drop cap, *so-called because its baseline drops below that of the first line of text in the paragraph. To create a drop cap, the typesetting system has to alter line leading to accommodate the oversized letter and create an indent that is canceled after a specified number of lines.*

for instance—needs to be more tightly letterspaced than smaller sizes of the same typeface. Whereas kerning affects the spacing between specific pairs of letters, changes to tracking affect the spacing of all letters.

Text-Formatting Capabilities

The third major source of quality in type lies in the ability of a typesetting system to arrange text elements on the page in very complex ways. The laser printer, like the commercial phototypesetting machine, has the potential to place any letter, in any size, anywhere on the page. This potential is limited only by the text-formatting information given to it. With the arrival of the laser printer, the capabilities of word processing programs have evolved toward those of typesetting programs. This is a great step forward, but the way these abilities have been organized and integrated into these programs is still rather primitive. By trying to make text formatting conceptually easy, programmers have usually compromised typographic control.

For instance, many advanced word processing programs now on the market make the user go through a series of menus to assign typographic attributes to text. The parameters in one menu may pertain to the entire document, another set to paragraphs, and yet another to individual characters and words. These arbitrary divisions are very limiting. Typically, line spacing is assigned as a paragraph attribute, which means it cannot be changed within a paragraph, making something as simple as the oversized initial capital letter (called a *drop cap*) in Figure 3-3 tedious if not impossible.

Trying to accomplish too much with limited tools means a lot of time spent trying to wring the most out of them. For the occasional publisher this may be acceptable, but for professional-looking results on a production schedule, professional tools are called for.

Chapter 4

Typesetting Fundamentals

The craft of typesetting goes back over 500 years to Gutenberg's development of movable type. In the ensuing centuries of handset type many of the concepts and much of the terminology of typography came into being—ideas and words that may no longer have any physical connection to how type is set today.

The fundamental measurements of typography are *picas* and *points*. These are absolute measurements that have fixed, standard values. Picas and points were developed as standards in the last century, but several groups proposed conflicting standard values, and what exists in typography today is a measuring system that doesn't really correspond to any other. An American pica is now defined as equaling .166040 inch—about $1/6$ of an inch. A point is $1/12$ of a pica—about $1/72$ of an inch. The correspondence between picas and inches is close—close enough to tempt people to regard it as absolute, but not close enough to allow for really accurate conversion. Although the inaccuracy is very small, the cumulative error over the width or length of a page can raise havoc when you're laying out pages.

Typographers deal almost exclusively in picas and points. The fineness of the measurements is well suited to the meticulous nature of the work. Inches are too coarse, and centimeters, although popular in Europe, are rarely used in the American publishing industry.

Type Size and Leading

Gutenberg's movable type is based on casting each letter of the alphabet on its own individual metal block. The raised image of the letter is inked, and the ink is offset onto the paper, forming the printed image. Many of these blocks are placed in rows

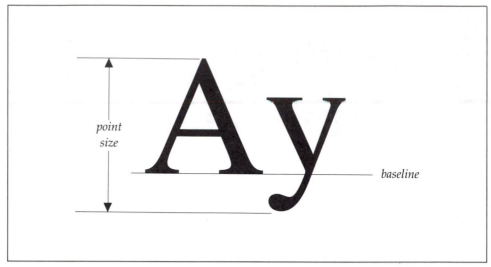

Figure 4-1 *The point size of a typeset character is roughly equal to the distance from the top of a typeface's tallest character to the bottom of the character that extends farthest below the baseline, the imaginary line upon which uppercase characters sit.*

to form lines of words, and the rows are stacked one above another to assemble pages. Perimeter braces press in from the sides, holding the made-up pages in square blocks.

The width of each letter block corresponds to that character's required escapement on a modern typewriter, printer, or typesetting machine. The height of each block is called its point size. If the height of a given alphabet's blocks is 12 points, that type is said to be 12-point type. (A common shorthand notation for this is 12'.) Because each letter has to fit on the face of its block, this height is equal to the distance from slightly above the top of its tallest letter (an *l* or any capital letter) to slightly below the bottom of its deepest letter, typically a *y* or *g* (see Figure 4-1). The little bit of extra space above and below the actual letterform is added to prevent the printed characters of one line from touching the characters in lines above or below it. Nowadays, the blocks are gone, but the concept remains the same, and the type size of a given character is roughly equal to the distance from *ascender* (the upward extension on letters such as *d* or *b*) to *descender* (the "tail" on a *y* or *q*).

Because these letter blocks were made out of lead alloy, vertical distances on a page were reckoned in terms of how much lead was used, hence the term *leading*, which is the typographer's word for vertical distance on the page. Consider as an example the 12-point type described above. All of the letter blocks for a 12-point

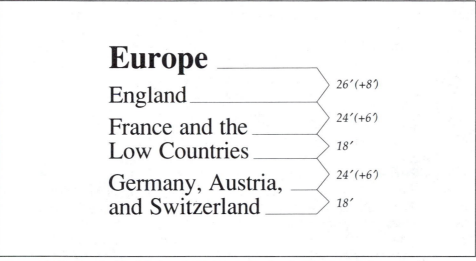

Europe

England — 26′ (+8′)

France and the — 24′ (+6′)
Low Countries — 18′

Germany, Austria, — 24′ (+6′)
and Switzerland — 18′

Figure 4-2 Leading for all of the type in this illustration is set at 18 points. From this basic setting, lead is added to provide extra space between items. The word England, for instance, is set with 8 points of extra lead, for a net line leading of 26 points. The alternative to the three extra lead commands used here is to change the leading for each and every line.

alphabet would be 12 points tall. When setting rows of this type, the hand typesetter has the option of stacking the lines of type directly on top of each other—setting them "solid"—or separating the lines with thin metal strips—"adding lead." This mechanical assembly of movable type provides the terminology still in use today.

On the typeset page, there is no evidence of those blocks, so leading is measured from the *baseline* of one typeset line to that of the line above it, as shown in Figure 4-2. In the case of solid-set type, that distance would be 12 points. To describe this to a typesetter, you write 12/12 (read "12 on 12"), meaning 12-point type set on 12 points of lead. If a typographer using movable type were to add a one-point-thick lead strip between the lines, he would be adding one point of leading, a condition expressed as 12/13.

Relative Measurements

Proportion is a very important aspect of type. Because typography is a predominantly visual system, issues of balance, proportion, and size ratios become very important considerations. For this reason, typography relies heavily on relative measurements: units of measure that have no absolute value, but whose values fluctuate in keeping with a fixed relationship to the prevailing point size. Relative measurements make it much easier to talk about type specifications without regard to specific numeric measurements.

The most fundamental of these relative units is the *em*. As its name implies, it is derived from the width of the letter *M*, usually the widest letter in a typeface's character set. Because the size of an em is tied to character width, the absolute value of an em changes as type size changes. Fortunately, this relationship is an easy one to remember: the width of an em is always equal to the point size of the type being used. In 12-point type, an em is 12 points wide. When using 30-point type, an em is 30 points wide.

The character-width measuring systems that control escapement (discussed in Chapter 4) are generally described in units per em. A 54-unit system, then, divides an em into 54 units, and a 100-unit system has 100 units per em, making it the potentially more precise of the two. These small measurements are usually called *typesetter units,* and they are used not only to express character widths precisely, but also to measure minute kerning adjustments between letters. Naturally, their definition in terms of the em makes them relative units as well. This means that one table of kerning information will work over a wide range of sizes: the space adjustment is expressed as a ratio of the set character size. If, say, millimeters were used to express these adjustments, a unique table of adjustments would have to be created for every point size used, because smaller characters need to be moved in smaller absolute amounts than large characters.

Fixed Spaces

Ems are most commonly used as expressions of escapement (horizontal space). A two-em paragraph indent, then, can be said to have been created by starting the first line with two em spaces. The nice thing about using ems for paragraph indents is that the proportion of indent size to text size remains constant even though point sizes may change throughout the text.

Em spaces are nonetheless referred to as "fixed spaces." This may seem contradictory, but they get this name to distinguish them from word spaces (known in typesetting as *spacebands*) and interletter spaces, which can be stretched or compressed during some typographic procedures and so cannot be relied on to have a specific width under all circumstances. A familiar example of this is in newspapers, where letter and word spacing is often exaggerated in order to make a line of type completely fill the column width. Fixed spaces are immune to this distortion, so that a 12-point em space will always measure exactly 12 points no matter how much the rest of the line may have been stretched or compressed.

Several other fixed spaces are in common use, and they too are linked to the point size in effect when they are called. One is the *en*, which is equal to one half of an em. Smaller yet is the *thin space*, which is user-definable on most typesetting systems; it is usually approximately equal to a standard word space, which makes it equal to roughly half an en, or one quarter of an em.

Another fixed space is the numeral space. Most typefaces assign identical character widths to all the numerals, 0 through 9. This allows these characters to align in neat columns in work such as financial tables. The numeral space is equal to this numeral width, allowing you to use it as a placeholder to create tidy columnar alignment of numbers.

What a Typesetting System Does

A typesetting system consists of three main parts. The *front end* consists of a computer and the typesetting programs. The *driver* is a program that translates the information from the front end into a language that can be understood by the third element in the equation, the *marking engine*—the typesetting machine or printer. A word processing system uses essentially the same system structure.

In some systems, the marking engine does little beyond taking instructions and creating drawings of characters out of information stored in its memory. These are referred to as "slave machines." Others, including most laser printers, do substantial computing of their own. Some printers and typesetting machines use a *page description language* to describe how marks should be placed on the typeset page. A page description language provides a common tongue by which many applications can describe printed output. These page description languages often work within the printer or typesetting machine itself, which means that a great deal of computing occurs within the printer. Sometimes the page description language is housed in an intermediate device (called a *raster image processor*) in which data from the front end is compiled into images of pages that the marking engine can then produce. In a networked system, the raster image processor is commonly shared by many computers. In high traffic systems, though, separate processors are sometimes placed in individual computers to avoid bottleneck delays as many operators try to process jobs at the same time.

Most of the formatting that determines the look of typeset matter is added by the keyboarder, but systems typically allow the operator to establish a set of default parameters that are automatically enacted for every job. These background functions save having to define every type parameter for every job. They define, for example, how the system will be allowed to modify spacebands to achieve justification, how fractions will be built, and how letter combinations will be kerned. Many of these parameters don't change very often—if at all—and they can be set just once to establish the general look of the type to the user's specifications. Most, however, can be overridden by the keyboarder as the occasion requires.

Bodoni developed lofty ideals and visualized anew the intrinsic beauty of typography. He introduced a distinct and beautiful style into his types that was the forerunner of all modern faces.

Flush left (rag right)

One changes which Bodoni introduced into the forms of roman letters was in the serifs. Those of the capitals he reduced to sharp lines of about the same weight as the thin strokes of the letters.

Flush right (rag left)

The serifs in Bodoni's lowercase characters are raised to an almost horizontal position at right angles with the upright strokes of the letters.

Centered (rag center)

Bodoni's style was always chaste, relying on on suitable spacing, good proportions, proper margins, and clean presswork, rather than upon decorative effects in vogue.

Justified

Figure 4-3 *In flush left type, the typesetting program fits as much text on each line as it can within the specified measure and then places any leftover space at the right margin. In flush right text, the extra space is placed at the left margin; in centered text the space is evenly divided at both ends of each line. In justified text, the extra space is divided evenly among the word spaces on each line; systems can usually be set to distribute some of this space between letters as well.*

Hyphenation and Justification

One of the principle tasks of the front-end computer is to determine where to break lines of text, a process called *hyphenation and justification*, or h&j, for short. Justification is the process of filling lines with type—both characters and spaces—and the program uses hyphenation as a device to make sure that as many letters as possible are put on each line.

Some confusion arises around the word *justified* as it applies to typography. This is because the term is used to describe columns of type that have straight vertical margins on both right and left, as in this book, making each line of type exactly the same length.

By contrast, type can be set in a variety of *ragged* styles, as shown in Figure 4-3. The names of these styles derive from which margin gets the ragged treatment (e.g., ragged right), which margin gets the vertically straight margin (flush left), or both (flush left, ragged right).

As far as the computer is concerned, though, all type is justified—the margin style merely determines where leftover space will be placed after as many letters as possible have been set on one line. Each line, then, is filled to the specified length using a combination of letters and spaces.

The primary factor in making end-of-line decisions is, of course, the line length, or *measure*, specified by the keyboarder. Other factors that must be considered include indents, typeface, margin treatment, type size, kerning, tracking, and hyphenation rules. In determining how best to fill a line with type, the program first determines the maximum line length allowed and whether it has to fill that measure completely (as with justified margins) or whether it can end the line short of the right margin (as in ragged right copy or on the last line of a paragraph). It determines what typeface and size are being used (and keeps track of changes and their ramifications); it then refers to a table of character widths used for that typeface so that it knows how much escapement to accord each character. It modifies this escapement based on overall tracking specifications; and for each and every two-letter combination, the program refers back to a table of kerning information and makes interletter spacing adjustments as necessary.

As the program assembles and measures the line from left to right, it comes into a zone in which it must decide where to end the line. The program will always try to fill the line as much as possible, and the default settings established by the operator create the rules for doing so. First the program looks to the restrictions the user has placed upon overall white space to see how much it can expand or contract spacebands. The program will try to end lines between words, but given the limitations placed on white space expansion and compression, this is not always possible.

Often the only allowable breakpoint for a line falls in the middle of a word. In this case, the program uses its hyphenation tools. It will look at the word that is straddling the margin and make a hyphenation decision based on a dictionary entry or, lacking that, on programmed logic rules, often called hyphenation algorithms. (Various methods used by h&j programs are described below.) The program repeats this task over and over for every line in the job. Because ending a number of consecutive lines with hyphens is visually distracting, most h&j programs allow you to place a limit on the number of consecutive hyphens that are permissible.

After h&j, the program will display the text on screen with the actual line breaks that will appear in the typeset output. In a mode called *measured h&j*, the display can be augmented by information that may include the lengths in picas and points of every line, the distance of each line from the top of the job, whether hyphenation has been based on a dictionary or a logic program, and whether a line is setting too loose, when, for instance, the program has been unable to abide by the specified spacing rules. These measurements can indicate whether the type is going to fit a layout even before any type is actually set.

About Hyphenation Routines

A typesetting program should be able to hyphenate automatically—it is the key to effective justification. The ability to hyphenate allows the computer to fill lines of type with minimal distortion of spaceband and letter space widths. In ragged margin columns, hyphenation can often be dispensed with, because lines are allowed to end short of the margin. But even in ragged copy, hyphenation becomes necessary in narrow measures; ending lines only at spacebands can result in a very irregular margin.

Making a hyphenation routine effective and efficient is a difficult task. It has to cope with an enormous number of words, and searching through a dictionary is a time-consuming task. Programs take many different approaches to hyphenation, some much better than others.

A whole-word reference dictionary—one that contains whole words and information on where they may be hyphenated—would, naturally, be the most effective hyphenation tool. The main problem with that is one of sheer bulk. The memory demands placed on a computer holding a large whole-word dictionary takes up room needed for other programs. Likewise, a massive dictionary can make searching for a word a very lengthy process.

The first hyphenation programs for microcomputers were based on spelling checkers, which are small whole-word dictionaries. Many of these spelling checkers cum hyphenators are still around, but they are not very effective or efficient. They generally have sacrificed completeness for speed—and they still don't end up being very fast.

Whole-word dictionaries may become more popular as computer memory becomes cheaper and microcomputers can address more and more of it quickly. For the time being, though, they are best reserved as backups to other hyphenation systems. Most good hyphenation programs will allow you to append a list of whole words onto whatever hyphenation system they use. This is feasible because you are unlikely ever to add so many words that you place a burden on the program.

Root hyphenation dictionaries take an approach similar to whole-word dictionaries, but they save space and speed searching by using only parts of words. In this way they can reduce redundant dictionary entries, letting one entry serve for many words with the same root construction. Such a root dictionary might include the entry *ac-com-pl-*, for instance, which can serve as a guide for the hyphenation of accomplice, accomplish, accomplishment, accompli, and accomplished.

With one root serving for many words, the size of the dictionary the computer must use is drastically diminished. In addition, a good root dictionary is supplemented by prefix and suffix information that will allow it to create hyphenation points farther along in the word than the root alone discloses. In the above example, the root plus the suffix information will allow *accomplishment* to be hyphenated at three points: *ac-com-plish-ment*. Even with this shortcut, however, root hyphenation dictionaries are rare outside the world of commercial typography. Creating an efficient look-up routine is still a very sophisticated piece of programming.

Another hyphenation strategy calls for making hyphenation decisions based on the detection of prefixes and suffixes. At first look, this seems like a very effective way to create a simple yet fairly effective hyphenation routine. English, being a Latin-based language, relies very heavily on a rather small collection of prefixes and suffixes to build words. A closer look, though, reveals a lot of shortcomings to this approach. Take the word *pressed*, for instance. It is a one-syllable word that a prefix/suffix program has a hard time with it can be hyphenated neither after *pre* nor before the *ed*.

The fourth common hyphenation method is the use of logic programs. Logical hyphenation can be remarkably effective, depending on the ability of the programmer who wrote the routine. Logic-based hyphenation programs take prefixes and suffixes one step further, analyzing the structures of words to look for rules that allow or preempt hyphenation. Such a rule might be allowing hyphenation between consecutive consonants, as in *pillage, collect, assemble,* or *calligraphy*. Like the prefix/suffix routine mentioned previously, though, it's not going to have an easy time with a word like *pressed*.

The shortcomings of all of these systems demand some kind of safety net, and that is the user-definable *exception dictionary*. Such a facility allows you to add specific words to the hyphenation routine when it becomes evident that the program can't cope with them by its own devices. Exception dictionaries are always placed in the program so that they are consulted first.

A good hyphenation routine, then, does not depend on any one of the above methods, but on a combination of them. A typical configuration relies first on a whole-word or root dictionary. If a clear answer to the hyphenation problem at hand is not available there, the program will proceed to a logic back-up based on prefixes, suffixes, and a hyphenation algorithm built from the rules of word construction. Failing that, it will refuse to hyphenate at all, which usually results in a very loose line or a large gap in the right-hand margin.

Words that the system can't hyphenate well become apparent during proofreading. These troublesome words should be added to the exception dictionary to prevent them from being stumbling blocks in the future. Some words, though, present special problems. Words like *produce* and *record* hyphenate differently depending on whether they are being used as nouns or verbs. To deal with these, programs are now coming to market that use artificial intelligence programming techniques to attempt to divine the usage of such words from their surrounding text.

Composition

After h&j, pretypeset copy is sent through a composition program, in which all of the coding information embedded in the text by the keyboarder and the h&j program is translated into a language that the marking engine can understand. Because different typesetting machines understand different languages, the composition program must be tailored to a specific marking engine. The composed file contains all of the information the typesetting machine needs to create the final output.

In commercial typography, composition programs have been complicated by the lack of any standards. Each manufacturer has traditionally based its system on proprietary hardware and software. This means that a front end manufacturer who wants the largest possible number of clients must create drivers for a wide range of marking engines. These relationships make for many awkward and expensive translation procedures.

As mentioned earlier, a new generation of device-independent page description languages that position themselves between front end computers and typesetting machines is evolving. Apart from creating a kind of graphic and typographic Esperanto that all systems can understand, though, these languages do little to alter the fundamental relationship between front end and marking engine.

At the heart of this relationship is shared font information. In order for the computer to perform h&j, it must have a complete set of character widths for every typeface in the job. The same information must be available to the typesetting machine as well in order for its output to correspond to what the h&j program has so painstakingly measured. In addition, the typesetting machine must also have all the data needed to create images of all the characters in all the typefaces called for in the job.

For the microcomputer and laser printer to act as a typesetting system, they must emulate this relationship, and if phototypeset output is to remain an option, the phototypesetting machine also needs identical information. The practical ramifications of these relationships are discussed in Chapter 8.

Chapter 5

The Language of Typesetting

The typesetting machine does whatever it's told to do—the typographer's responsibility is to completely describe the look of the output, and this is the job of typographic formatting.

As described in Chapter 4, there are three basic strategies for formatting text using computers: embedding typographic codes in the text; using typographic style sheets that hold formatting information for standard text elements (captions, body text, headlines, and so on); and using on-screen menus of typographic options for interactive, WYSIWYG formatting.

Most commercial typesetting systems rely on the first system: some form of embedded coding. This method is similar to that employed by many word processing programs, including some of the old standbys such as MicroPro's WordStar. In such a system, the formatting instructions are keyed in directly by the keyboarder and appear on the computer's screen in the midst of the text stream. Typically, there is some kind of delimiter used as a preface to the code statement so the computer knows where text ends and formatting instructions begin.

One major advantage of such a system is that all of the typographic attributes of the text can be read directly from the screen display—nothing is hidden from the keyboarder. Such a system is particularly useful for formatting text that does not have standard, predefined styles—where type specifications change often, such as in advertising typography. Another benefit of an embedded code system is that all codes can be located and altered automatically using a simple search and replace utility common to most computer programs. Many WYSIWYG programs that run on microcomputers cannot execute such a search because there are no coding keystrokes to search for—the only thing visible on the screen is the result of formatting that is carried out in another part of the program. Formatting by style sheet is a more automated process than the code-as-you-go method described above. In this approach, all of the elements of a document—text, subheads, captions, etc.—are given generic tags—when you look at the document on the computer screen, the only coding that shows are these tags. Each of these tags has a set of typographic attributes associated with it, recorded in the so-called style sheet. Among word processors, the leading proponent of this approach is Microsoft Word for IBM PC's and compatible computers.

When a typesetting system uses such a scheme, the computer refers to the appropriate style sheet for its typographic formatting information during h&j. If type specifications change under such a system, the changes need to be registered in only one place—the style sheet. You don't need to edit the document to change typographic information. Separating formatting code from the copy allows typesetting novices to format documents using generic text element labels, and the documents can be output on any equipment once an appropriate style sheet is created.

Just as embedded coding schemes are most useful when typographic specifications change often and unpredictably within a document, style-sheet formatting is best for long, structured documents in which all of the text elements can be identified and labeled in advance. This makes them ideal for batch pagination processes, in which all of the typographic attributes of text blocks and pages are predefined and the computer lays out pages automatically by referring to its style guides.

Simple batch paginators automatically end each page after a specified number of lines. More complex batch pagination programs can automatically place footnotes and graphics on the page on which they are referenced, avoid ending a page with the first line of a paragraph (called an *orphan*), make sure subheads fall in acceptable parts of the page, and carry out a host of other page makeup decisions, all based on predefined style sheets.

The third typical text-formatting scheme can be seen as a combination of the previous two. In such a system, text formatting is interactive—that is, the keyboarder formats the text manually, but the typographic attributes are specified in program menus that drop down over the screen and then recede after the specification information has been inserted by the keyboarder. The results of the specifications appear on the screen in a style that mimics final typeset output. This is the standard modus operandi of programs running on Apple's Macintosh computers.

The benefits of this approach are its ease of use (because there are no codes to remember), its flexibility (it can function on a code-as-you-go basis, like embedded coding schemes), and its WYSIWYG display, which allows the keyboarder to preview on the computer's screen the layout of the type to be output.

These distinct ways of working will not stay separate for long—in fact, hybrid approaches that feature the ability to switch back and forth between different formatting schemes are already beginning to appear. No one of them is best for all applications. It is likely that page-oriented type shops—those doing short, typographically demanding jobs, such as ads, brochures, and annual reports—will continue working with the embedded code systems because of the fine control and high performance they provide. Those doing books, technical documentation, directories, and other lengthy works—the document-oriented typographers—will prefer the batch systems that feature more automated typesetting and page makeup. The interactive WYSIWYG systems, meanwhile, will continue to be the province of those who need the design control and ease of use they offer.

Assembling a Toolbox

Typographic flexibility depends on a basic set of formatting commands. Outlined here is a solid set of typographic capabilities that are important to quality text-formatting. The list here outlines a basic set of text-formatting tools necessary to set professional-looking type. The terminology used is borrowed from commercial typesetting, and it may differ slightly from system to system—especially on microcomputer systems emphasizing "user friendliness"—but all these capabilities should be present in any sound typographic package.

These features can be grouped into several major divisions. One of these groups is line-ending commands. You should be able to set an individual line flush left, flush right, centered, or indented whenever you want, regardless of the status of surrounding text.

A strong typesetting program should also feature a wide variety of automatic indention schemes that can be combined to create layouts with very elaborate shapes. It is also important to have a good tabular package for setting tables, charts, and columnar matter. A program should also offer control over escapement and spacing, letting you place letters and text precisely on the page.

Some special effects are also very important. These include automatic fraction building, horizontal and vertical rules, control over character width, and automatic as well as discretionary hyphenation.

The discussions that follow of many of these typographic controls include examples of their implementations. In these examples, the commands used to format the text are set in a contrasting typeface and set off by angle brackets, like so: [change point size to 14].

The Fundamental Parameters

Formatting text to be typeset doesn't have to be complicated, although it often turns out that way. In truth, there are only five parameters a system needs to have defined in order to set type: typeface, type size, line length, margin handling, and leading. This information is sufficient to produce running lines of text.

The typesetting system must know what typeface is going to be used so that it can refer to the correct character-width table when it carries out h&j. Accordingly, it must also know what point size is called for, so it can gauge escapement correctly. You must also specify line measures and how margins will be handled, whether the text will be set flush left, flush right, justified, or centered. The fifth fundamental parameter is line leading, and with leading you begin to see how type parameters are interconnected and interdependent.

In designing text, you should make it as easy as possible for the reader to scan back to the left margin to pick up the beginning of the next line after reaching the end of the one before. The closer the lines are together, the more difficult this task becomes for the reader. Over narrow line measures in the neighborhood of 10 to 13 picas—like in newspaper columns—the eye finds the next line easily, even if the lines are set solid, with no extra leading. The wider the measure, though, the more help the eye needs in finding its place at the left margin. Opening up the leading a little helps the eye by creating very thin horizontal bands of white space between the lines—bands that the eye can follow easily from margin to margin.

At the column measure used in this book, we have added two points of leading between lines, setting this text 10/12 (10 on 12). Had we chosen a wider column measure on the same size page, it is likely that we would have chosen to add three points of lead and set the text 10/13. This would aid the eye and also keep the all-text page from looking gray and uninviting.

With computer typesetting has come a capability impractical with metal type: *negative leading*, in which the leading value is less than the type's point size. This means, for example, that 12-point type can be set on 11 points of lead. For text set in capitals and lowercase, this will probably mean that the ascenders of one line will collide with the descenders of the line above it—not a very pleasing effect. But since capital letters have no descenders, all-capital material can be very tightly spaced by using negative leading. Negative leading is used very often in advertising typography to create special effects or to cram a maximum number of words into a limited space (see Figure 5-1).

The increments in which leading can be defined vary from system to system, but half-point increments are typical, and some systems also work in quarters or tenths of points. The limitation here is often the typesetting machine, especially if it is a 300 dpi laser printer.

Line-Ending Commands

Line-ending commands in typesetting are much more varied than in word processing, which usually depends on the Return/Enter key. Many word processors

Figure 5-1 *The word SALE has been set on negative lead—its leading is less than its point size. If the line above it were not set in all capitals, the descenders of lowercase letters would overlap with the line below. The smaller letters in the top line were set with reverse lead to raise them off the baseline and align the tops of the larger* L *and* Y.

define paragraphs as all text matter enclosed between two carriage returns, which means that any manual line break (a Return) within that paragraph will also create a new paragraph. Typesetting systems use a variety of commands to specify line breaks. The major ones are described here. The flexibility afforded by this variety is a key to a productive typesetting system.

Quads   To understand the concept of quads, it is best to return to the days of hand-set type. Quads were small metal blocks that were used to fill out lines of type that did not fill their full line length—the quads took up space to keep all the blocks chocked tightly into their page frames. Because they did not reach up to the printing plane of the alphabet characters, they generated blank space on these lines. Last lines of paragraphs, which usually didn't run to the full measure, then, were packed with quads to hold the letter blocks in place. These quads could be used to center lines of type or to align then flush right or flush left. The jargon remains today: quad left, quad right, quad center.

In computer typesetting, these three quad commands are line-ending commands, and they can be used in a number of ways. A quad command tells the computer, "End the current line here, and quad it in the direction indicated." The three quad commands override general instructions about margin treatment. In other words, the keyboarder can tell the system to set all text flush left, but the moment the system sees a quad right command, it will end the current line and set it flush right. Then it will return to its business of setting flush left copy.

Examples:

This block of text demonstrates the effects of the quad commands. Although this is a justified paragraph, as soon as a quad command is encountered [quad left]
the current line is ended, and whatever portion of the line the h&j program has
been able [quad right]
to fill up to that point is pushed to the margin indicated by the quad command. Only the line in which the quad command occurs is so affected. The next line will
be set according to the prevailing margin specifications.[quad center]

End Paragraph   An end-paragraph command is also a line-ending command, but with fewer specific ramifications than the quads. An end-paragraph command will also end the line immediately, but it doesn't require the keyboarder to specify in what direction that line should be quadded—this command will refer back to the margin treatment parameter in effect and quad appropriately. When text is being set flush left, it will quad the line left; if text is setting centered, an end-paragraph command will quad the last line to the center.

In addition to this automatic quadding feature, the end-paragraph command acts as a trip wire for many other typesetting commands (primarily those affecting paragraph formatting style), toggling some on, others off. Typesetting programs can establish commands that arrange for the automation of some paragraph-for-matting commands, and the end-paragraph command announces the end of one paragraph and the beginning of a new one.

Indention

Indention encompasses all variations from the stated line measure. (Indentation is what you get on the door of your car if it's hit by a rock—indention is what you get if you move the first line of a paragraph in from the margin.)

Commercial typesetting systems feature a wide range of indention styles designed to be used individually, in conjunction with others, or in special situations. The names given to these indents vary from system to system, usually because program designers are struggling to give them names that create easy-to-remember mnemonic labels, like *IF* for Indent First or *IL* for Indent Left. The following descriptions are based on more generic names, chosen to be as descriptive as possible.

Standing Indent   A standing indent moves the left or right margin (or both at once) toward the center of the text column. Once a standing indent is invoked it stays in place until the keyboarder turns it off. This may not seem remarkable, but most typesetting indents are conditional and automatically toggle off under certain conditions—commonly at the appearance of an end-paragraph command. It is important, then, that the keyboarder has available an indent that is not vulnerable to any other changing conditions. This indent will stay in effect regardless of how many lines are set, how many paragraphs come and go, or how many other indents are created and canceled. Whatever else happens, a standing indent will stand until the keyboarder specifically cancels it.

Paragraph Indent   The paragraph indent works very much like the standing indent—it moves the left or right margin of each line of text that follows it in toward the center of the typeset column. The important difference is that this indent is canceled by an end-paragraph command. This is a great insurance policy against accidentally leaving in place an indent that was intended to be only temporary.

First-line indent   Often called *indent first*, this command tells the typesetting machine, "Indent the first line after an end-paragraph command." This allows the keyboarder to automatically indent the first line of every paragraph by a specifiable amount. The command can be inserted at the beginning of a long passage of running text, and as long as each paragraph is ended with an end-paragraph command, the first line of the next paragraph will automatically be indented by the specified amount. The paragraph indents throughout this book were generated by an indent-first command and actuated by an end-paragraph command at the end of every paragraph. Where paragraph indents were not desired—as in the paragraph that follows this one—quad lefts were used to end the preceding paragraphs.

Hanging Indent   A hanging indent is the functional opposite of the indent-first command, and it, too, is activated by the end-paragraph command. The hanging indent command says, "Set the first line after an end-paragraph command without any indention, but indent all of the rest of the lines in the paragraph."

Hanging indents are useful in directory listings—the phone book is a typical example—where almost every line is an independent text element. Hanging indents are used to distinguish those lines that are continuations of the previous line, not a new item.

Example:

[end paragraph][cancel first-line indent][18′ hanging indent]
The command string for this paragraph shows the interaction of indention codes. The first line of text following it sets flush, and the rest are indented. Because the end-paragraph that triggers the hanging indent also causes the first-line indent to be activated, the latter must be turned off.

Counting Indent   Counting indents allow the keyboarder to create an indent or a series of indents that remain in effect for a specified number of lines, take effect only after a certain number of lines, or both.

Example:

[indent the next two lines 0′, then the following five lines 18′]
Because the keyboarder does not know where lines will break during the h&j process, these indents call for the computer to do the line counting and create indents as required. This command can be used, for example, to create a *runaround indent* into which an illustration will be inserted. This command can tell the typesetting machine, "Count down x number of lines, then set an indent of y points from the left margin, let that indent stand for z lines, then cancel the indent." These counting indents can be set from the left margin, the right margin, or both at the same time. A good typesetting system will allow very complex counting indents, with 20 or more consecutive indents included in the same command.

Skewed Indent   Skewed indents let the keyboarder create straight-line margins that run at angles from the normal vertical margins. Using the counting indent described above, a skew could be created by a command that says, "Indent one line 1 pica, then indent one line 2 picas, then indent one line 3 picas" and so on, with each succeeding line indented an additional pica. A true skewed indent specifies the beginning point of the angled margin and its terminus with one, much simpler, command.

Example:

[set ten-line skew, ten pica indent on the fifth line]
The end points of the skewed margin can be expressed in terms of lines of text and indents from the margin, as in the command string above. Alternatively, they may be expressed in absolute distances on the page, as in, "Start the indent 14 picas from the top of the page and 4 picas from the left edge; end it 33 picas from the top of the page and 11 picas from the left edge." These absolute page coordinates are useful for shaping type around artwork, especially when you're experimenting with different type specifications. Either method gives the computer two points on the page: the starting point and the ending point for the angled margin. The computer draws an imaginary line between these two points that acts as the new margin and creates the appropriate indents automatically for each line. Skews, like most other indents, can work from either margin or both at once.

Spot Indent   The spot indent command does not rely on any stated units of measure; rather, it creates an indent starting wherever it is inserted. This is a very handy command for instances in which an indent is to be based on the width of typeset matter, not on a measurement expressed in picas and points. When using this kind of indent, it isn't necessary for you to know how wide a piece of text is in order to create an indent customized exactly to its width. Furthermore, if the type size for the job needs to be changed, the indent will change automatically, because it is fixed to a position relative to text, not a position expressed in absolute measurements. This is also a very useful indent for creating precise alignment in outline formats, where successive levels of indention rely on the widths of numbers or letters used to signify the various levels within the outline.

Example:

Hamlet: [spot indent]To be or not to be, that is the question. Whether 'tis nobler in the heart to suffer the slings and arrows of outrageous fortune...

creates:

Hamlet: To be or not to be, that is the question. Whether 'tis nobler in the heart to
         suffer the slings and arrows of outrageous fortune...

Tabular Commands

Tabular work in commercial typography is substantially different from that in word processing. Tabs in typesetting systems are a complex agglomeration of indention commands, allowing great flexibility in formatting. The capabilities of tabular utilities in typesetting programs vary widely and can be very complex.

In typesetting systems, each tab column, or *tab field*, has defined margins, just like any other column of text. This means that if you try to fit a 14-pica-long sentence into a 10-pica-wide tab field, that text will be wrapped, winding up on two lines within the column. This makes vertical alignment in tables very complex, because the computer has to remember on which baseline to align the text in the following tab column. Depending upon the sophistication of the program, this alignment of entries may be automatic, or it may require the keyboarder to leave position markers by which the computer can align successive entries. Clearly, the more automatic the alignment, the better.

These rigid tab boundaries have a couple of tremendous advantages over their word processing counterparts. First, runover lines don't have to be broken by hand—the machine does that automatically. Second, the entries for each column are entered in a logical sequence—left to right across the table, the lengths of their entries notwithstanding, and the computer places them on their correct tabs, properly aligned. The keyboarding is complex, but it is nothing compared to the very complex tasks being accomplished by the computer.

In setting tabs in a typesetting system, the keyboarder first defines the width of each of the tabular columns, making sure that their total width corresponds to the previously specified line measure. In all likelihood, the keyboarder will also specify *gutters* between the tab columns, to make sure that there is a vertical band of white space that will keep the columns distinct from one another. A 30-pica measure, for instance, may be divided into three 10-pica-wide tab columns, or into three 9-pica-wide tab columns with 1.5-pica gutters between the second and third columns. Text entered in the first column will wrap as needed within the tab field until the end of that tab entry is reached. A quad or tab-end command will then direct the computer to begin setting text at the second tab.

There are four basic tabular commands: one defines the number and widths of the tab columns and gutters; the second tells the computer, "This is the beginning of a tabular line—we are now setting in tabs;" the third says, "This marks the end of a tab entry—move on to the text tab column;" and the fourth says, "We are no longer setting in tabs—suspend (or forget) the tabular specifications stated earlier."

The powerful tabular programs in commercial typography can create tables like those seen in many corporate annual reports that include rules; single tabs that straddle several others below them; flush left, flush right, and centered tab entries; vertical rules in the gutters; tab entries aligned on a decimal point or another character; tabs defined automatically by the width of the text set in them; various forms of indention of entries within tabs; and a host of other complex forms of alignment and spacing.

Spacing Commands

Indention and margin commands establish the shapes of text blocks and their relationships to the page. Spacing commands establish the spatial relationships of the smaller text elements: lines, words, and letters. It is through the skilled use of these commands that typographers create the fine, highly readable type to which we've become accustomed.

Spaceband Control   Typesetting systems can create limits for the computer to work within when attempting to justify a line of type. A good spaceband-control facility can define the minimum, maximum and optimum value a spaceband should have. These provide the target the computer will try to match when laying down a line of type. Typically, in justified type, hyphenation alone is not sufficient to create a line that precisely fills the measure, so the system is forced to manipulate the width of the spacebands, trying to stay as close as possible to the specified optimum width. This creates a consistency of word spacing that results in the desirable even color across the page.

The value assigned to the spacebands should be in proportion to the overall tightness of the type being set. Some people prefer a looser set, and in those cases the spacebands should be widened slightly to create a spacing consistent with the prevailing character spacing.

Letterspacing   Usually, the spaces between letters are fixed, altered only by kerning commands. When *letterspacing* is allowed, the h&j program can expand spaces between letters (letter spaces) as well as spacebands (word spaces) when justifying a line of type. In general it is desirable to keep letterspacing ranges to a minimum, as wide spacing fluctuations give an uneven look to the type on the page. For very narrow column measures in justified mode—as in newspaper work—letterspacing is a very important tool for enabling the computer to justify lines. Letterspacing is also a useful design tool, and using it to stretch words to fill a given measure has become a popular graphic device.

Example:

[allow letterspacing][allow maximum spaceband width]Stretch this line.

creates:

S t r e t c h   t h i s   l i n e .

Tracking   Tracking adjustments proportionately alter the escapement accorded to every typeset character. Typesetting programs usually offer several tracking levels that are user-definable, and which vary the look of the type from loose letterspacing to tight letterspacing.

Tracking adjustment is a typographic response to the way the eye reacts to type in different sizes. 36-point type is proportionally three times larger than 12-point type—it is three times as tall and three times as wide, and letter spaces in 36-point type are three times as wide as in 12-point type. The eye perceives this differently, though, and letter spaces seem to grow proportionally faster than the letters themselves. This means that at larger type sizes, type appears to be set looser, with more white space between characters. To counteract this visual effect, tracking is typically tightened as type size increases—this is very evident in advertising typography, where very tight letterspacing is often evident in large type sizes. Tracking is also often varied in response to the appearance of certain typefaces. Very light and airy typefaces often get tighter tracking to make them look more solid on the page.

Unfortunately, it has become common practice for microcomputer typesetting and page makeup programs to boast automatic kerning, when the feature they are referring to is actually tracking control. Sometimes this is confusingly referred to as "track kerning," a hybrid concept that is quite deceptive. Kerning refers strictly to the adjustment of space between particular letter pairs, whereas tracking adjustments affect all letter spaces to the same degree. The first sample below shows a typical tracking setting for text-size type.

Examples:

[tracking level 1] Tracking

[tracking level 2] Tracking

[tracking level 3] Tracking

Kerning   Most kerning is done automatically in the computer during h&j. Commercial systems allow the user to assemble look-up tables of specific letter combinations and the spacing adjustments they require. Every typeface, because of its unique design and character widths, gets its own kern table. Commercial systems commonly allow the user to create over 1,000 kern pairs per typeface. This may seem like a huge number, but just among the uppercase and lowercase alphabets and a few common forms of punctuation there are over 2500 potential kerning pairs—and this doesn't include numerals and a host of common typographic symbols. For a quality commercial system, 800 kern pairs is probably a bare minimum. In a laser printer system, about half this number is probably adequate, because the low resolution of laser printer type masks the need for many fine adjustments. Because there is always a need for manual kerning, systems should also allow the keyboarder to control the kerning of specific letter combinations on-screen.

Examples:

Without kerning:
A Trip Down the Wabash River

With kerning:
A Trip Down the Wabash River

Position Commands

Freedom to place type with precision anywhere on the page is one key to a powerful typesetting system. This freedom should apply to blocks of text as well as individual characters, and it is especially important in display and creative typography, such as that commonly found in advertising work.

Extra Lead/Reverse Lead   The command that establishes the leading parameter defines the distance from the baseline of one line of type to the baseline of the one above it; extra lead and reverse lead commands create modifications to that basic leading scheme—they alter the position of the baseline for the remainder of that typeset line or until they're countermanded.

One of the most common applications for the extra lead command is providing extra space between paragraphs. If you're setting type on 14 points of lead and ask for extra lead of 14 points (also called a *line space*) at the beginning of a new paragraph, the first line of that paragraph will set on 28 points of lead. If you ask for 7 extra points of lead instead (or a *half-line space*), the first line of that paragraph will set on 21 points of lead. At the end of that typeset line, the system will return the leading to the specified 14 points.

Leading is one of the important frames of reference for the typographer when typesetting a page. Always knowing the position of the current baseline relative to the preceding one is a key to efficient and accurate placement of type. Throughout this book, we have been creating line spaces by adding lead.

Insert Space   The insert-space command allows you to insert a fixed amount of horizontal space. It can be used to create indents and gaps in text or to insert space between characters. Some programs use a variant of this command to lay down rules of specified lengths.

Example:

[change column width to 20 picas]
Joe Jones[insert 20′ space]Sam Smith[quad center]
[extra lead 6′][insert 60′ hairline rule][quad center]
[extra lead 6′]Attorneys at Law[quad center]
Franchise Consultants[quad center]

creates:

        Joe Jones   Sam Smith

          Attorneys at Law
        Franchise Consultants

Position Markers   These markers are used when working in multicolumn formats to designate vertical positions on the page. Two side-by-side columns of type can be aligned at the top by placing a marker on the first line of one column and returning to it to start the second column. Likewise, the last line in a column can be marked so that type set later can be positioned below it with precision.

Example:

[indent 16 picas from the right][mark position]This text will form itself into a narrow column by virtue of the indent from the right margin. When you have gone as far as you want to go in this column, you proceed to the next…[mark position of maximum depth][return to the marked position][cancel right indent][indent 16 picas from the left]and you start the second column with its top line base-aligned with the top line of the left column.[return to maximum depth][cancel indent][quad center]
[extra lead 5′]The end.[quad center]

creates:

This text will form itself into a narrow column by virtue of the indent from the right margin. When we have gone as far as we want to go in this column, we proceed to the next…

and we start the second column with its top line base-aligned with the top line of the left column.

The end.

X-Y Coordinates   X-Y coordinate positioning allows the keyboarder to specify the exact position on the page in which a piece of type will be placed. The X and Y refer, respectively, to horizontal and vertical positions on an imaginary grid that overlays the page. X-Y coordinates can be used to make up pages by establishing the positions for all of the text elements on a page. Each element on the page is given an address expressed in terms of its position on the X-Y grid, and the program automatically places the type at the specified point.

Additional Features

Because digital type fonts are stored as data, not as physical replicas of real letters, they are subject to mathematical manipulation, resulting in a number of special effects. Some common results are described below. Also included in this section are some common utilities that make commercial typesetting systems such powerful production tools.

Changing Character Widths   Depending on the nature of the fonts they use, many systems can distort typeset characters by setting them with the height of one point size and the width of another point size. The result is a hybrid character that appears either expanded or condensed. As you can see in the samples below, the proportions of the characters suffer somewhat as they are distorted, but you can achieve some striking effects with this simple device. Altering the set width of the text can help you with last minute copy fitting, as the a minor change can shorten a text passage with only a subtle change in the appearance of the type.

Example:

[change point size to 24'][change width to 36']

Here is some 24-point type set with 36-point character widths

[change point size to 24'][change width to 12']

and some 24-point type set with 12-point character widths.

Rules In typography, lines generated by the typesetting machine are called *rules*. Typesetting systems typically limit themselves to horizontal and vertical rules—no angles. The thicknesses of these rules are determined by the output device, and their lengths are controlled by specific numeric commands or *fill* commands (see below). Even though a typesetting system may provide only a limited number of rule thicknesses, these can be used as building blocks to create rules of virtually any thickness.

Character Fills Character fill commands are used to produce a long string of one particular character repeated over and over again. The distance between the characters is determined by commands that control letter and word spacing. The most common example of this is the use of leader dots, those horizontal lines of small dots or periods that typically appear in price lists, menus, catalogues, and tables of contents.

Underscores Typesetting underscore commands are very similar to word processing underscores, but a good typesetting system gives you control over the thickness of the rule and how far below the baseline it sets, and some will interrupt the underscore rule so that it doesn't collide with characters' descenders, which hang below the baseline.

Build Fractions   Fraction-building commands automatically convert numerals on either side of a slash (also called a *virgule* or *solidus*) or a specific character called a fraction bar into a fraction built from inferior and superior numerals. This command will automatically convert 5/8, for example, into ⁵/₈. Although fonts may include some prebuilt fractions, font manufacturers typically consider fraction building to be a responsibility of the composition software.

Formats   Formats are the big-league versions of the macro commands familiar to many microcomputer users—they are shorthand codes that represent strings of command sequences or text that reduce the need for repetitive keystrokes. These formats are created by the keyboarder and can be saved for future use in a specific job, a group of jobs, or all of the jobs created on the system.

Formats typically consist of one or more strings of command codes; when the format is called by the keyboarder, the string of commands is enacted. A format may consist of several command strings separated by *link* or *merge commands*. These link commands are like punctuation within formats; they tell the computer, "This is the end of the current command string; return to the text string until further notice." When the keyboarder gives the appropriate signal, the next portion of the format will be invoked. Formats can be nested one inside another, and extremely complicated command structures can be formed, with one format feeding back into another.

Chapter 6

Fonts and Typeface Selection

The visible difference between typewritten and "published" documents are the typefaces; the laser printer's ability to use commercial-style typefaces is the basis of desktop publishing. This chapter examines criteria for selecting and using typefaces in your documents. It discusses some aesthetic aspects of typeface selection and combination, but primarily it looks at type and typefaces in utilitarian ways: the functional components of typefaces, the different kinds of typefaces and how they are used, and how families of typefaces are built and how the members work with each other.

Fonts and Faces

The terms *font* and *typeface* have distinct meanings, although they are often used interchangeably. A typeface is a set of characters that share a common design that distinguishes the typeface from all other character sets. A font is the physical source from which that typeface is generated. (The word font comes from the same French root as *fountain*, with the implication of source, or wellspring; hence, that from which type is born.) First a typeface is designed, and then a font is manufactured that can generate the letter images of that typeface.

The essence, then, is this: A font is the matrix from which a face is generated. Letter Gothic and Courier are popular impact printer typefaces; the daisy wheels from which they are printed are fonts. Looking at a page of type, then, you can inquire, "What typeface is that?" or "What font was used to set that type?" but not "What font is that?" When fonts had more solid forms, the distinction was clear, and fonts were easily distinguished from the faces they represented. In the days

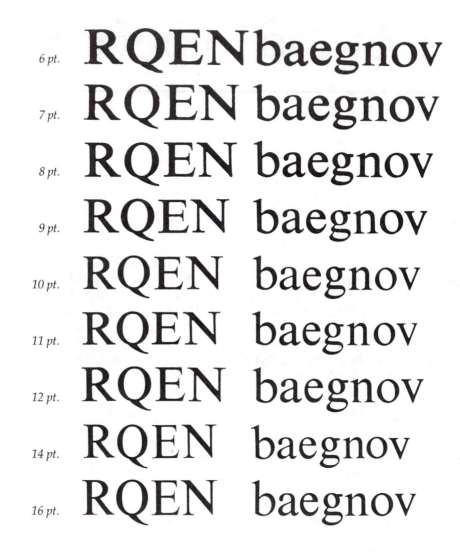

Figure 6-1 *These samples of Times Roman type demonstrate how typefaces have traditionally been uniquely designed for specific point sizes. Here, four sizes have been photographically enlarged to the same cap height to highlight these differences. At 6 point, the face has to be more hefty for optimum legibility, and as point size increases the characters can become more delicate. (Courtesy Bigelow & Holmes)*

a b c d e f g h i j k l mn o p q r s t

u v w x y z A B C D E F G H I J K L M N

O P Q R S T U V W X Y Z 1 2 3 4 5 6 7 8

9 0 / ; : ' $ %¢ & (—) ¨ * / , . ? ! ´

˘ ˷ † ¡ ˇ ` œ ı £ ^ [¯ · § ¿] ß ˜ æ ‡

f ø å – › ‹ « » fi fl „ " " ‰ Œ ÆØ Å

Figure 6-2 *The standard character set for a font from the Mergenthaler type*
library, shown here, has a maximum size of 128 characters. Recent changes in
computer architecture have begun to make 256-character fonts common. This gives
you the convenience of having to change fonts less often for various accents and
utility characters, but it has also increased the memory requirements of computers
that handle the larger fonts.

of hand-set metal type, characters were cast from master forms that were carved
individually for each type size. Type designers routinely made design alterations
in different sizes of one typeface to maintain a consistent level of readability over a
range of sizes. The stroke of an *l*, for instance, might look balanced and in proportion to other letters at 10 points, but when enlarged proportionally to 72 points, it
might appear too thick and clumsy (see Figure 6-1).

For this reason, every size of a typeface had its own "font master"—the set of
molds from which individual printing blocks were cast—each with a slightly different design. In old print shops, the set of printing blocks for each typeface was
kept in its own cabinet, and each size was allotted a font drawer. When a printer
specified a font, then, he was calling for a typeface and a type size. A particular job
might call for 10-point, 14-point, and 20-point Bodoni Bold: one typeface, three
fonts.

In early phototypesetting machines, type was set by flashing an intense light
through a glass or film negative. Type sizes were changed by lens manipulation, so

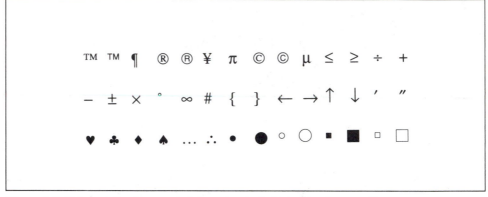

Figure 6-3 *This sampler of common pi characters includes serif and sans serif copyright and trademark symbols and various sized open and closed bullets and ballot boxes, in the lower right.*

many sizes could be generated from one negative (the font). Because there is a limit to the range that lenses can enlarge and shrink an image and still maintain the image's clarity, typesetters still had access to different font masters for different size ranges, but the distinction between font and face was already becoming blurred.

When digital type arrived, characters began to be generated electronically, and one master image of a character could be scaled to any point size. With just one font master per typeface, the terms *face* and *font* became virtually interchangeable. Although digital fonts still may have different master designs for different size ranges, these unique masters are invisible to the person setting the type; they are automatically engaged when the appropriate type size is invoked.

Interestingly, the advent of laser printers has revived size-specific fonts. Some desktop publishing systems do not allow the use of scalable fonts, so a separate font is required for each point size of a typeface used.

What Constitutes a Font?

Font manufacturers have different ideas about what should be included in a standard font. Figure 6-2 shows a typical character set from the Mergenthaler font collection (a leading commercial font library). Often the main font for a typeface is augmented by complementary fonts, which contain alternate characters, small capitals, old-style numbers, and unusual multilingual accents. The current trend, though, is toward larger fonts that include more characters, doing away with the need for complementary fonts.

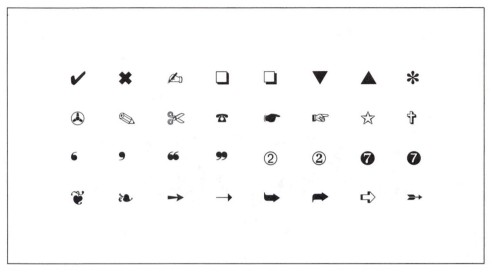

Figure 6-4 *Dingbats are pi characters marked by their decorative or whimsical quality. This selection is from a large collection designed by noted type designer Hermann Zapf.*

A font should include all of the characters and symbols for which design uniformity is important. Even seemingly generic characters such as periods and dashes have to be designed for each typeface. For a harmonious appearance, as many characters as possible should be designed and proportioned to match each other. In addition to the alphabetic and numeric characters, a font's character set should include all the major forms of punctuation (including opening and closing single and double quotation marks); common diacritical marks (tilde, umlaut, acute and grave accents); brackets, braces, and parentheses; em and en dashes; and a fraction bar for building fractions. Another helpful character to have available is a dotless *i* for use with accents, so that the accent doesn't collide with the dot in a word like naïve.

For seldom-used characters and symbols and for those for which design consistency is not so important, font manufacturers create *pi fonts,* which contain utility characters. A mathematics pi font, for instance, typically contains Greek characters; plus, equals, and minus signs; a multiplication sign (as opposed to a lowercase *x*); extra bracket styles; and other characters. Commercial typography pi fonts include common advertising symbols such as bullets, ballot boxes, check marks, and arrows (see Figure 6-3). Specialty pi fonts abound for fields including music, science, TV listings (those little screen shapes with the channel numbers inset), and horse-racing forms.

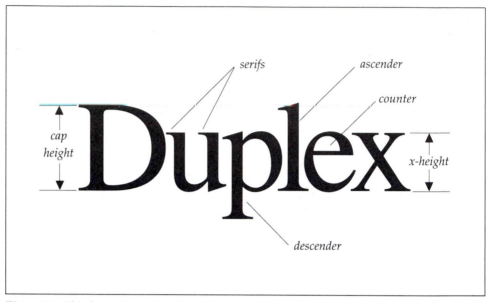

Figure 6-5 *This figure illustrates a few of the major features of typical roman characters. The legibility of characters is based in part on the proportions of cap height to x-height, the contrast between the thick and thin portions of letters, and the design of the serifs, which make it easy for the eye to differentiate and recognize letters.*

in addition to these pi fonts, font manufacturers also assemble fonts of decorative type elements called *dingbats.* These may be elements used for assembling borders or such novelty characters as smiling faces, flowers, little scissors (for "cutting on the dotted line"), stars, snowflakes, and other whimsical shapes (see Figure 6-4).

The ability to pick and choose among fonts is limited by the hardware and software you use for typesetting. Traditionally, manufacturers of computer type-setting machines have created their own font libraries, incompatible with typesetting machines from other suppliers. A move toward hardware-independent page description languages, such as Adobe Systems' PostScript, Xerox's Interpress, Imagen's DDL, and Donald Knuth's TeX, however, promises to provide common text-processing languages that let users of diverse systems use a common font library. It appears that the next few years will witness growing competition among page description languages as they vie for status as the industry standard. In all likelihood, we will not see a clear cut winner any time soon. This open marketplace is encouraging the formation of many new font companies who no longer have to be in the hardware business to sell their wares.

The Anatomy of Type

Figure 6-5 shows the basic parts of Western alphabetic characters and illustrates some of the fundamental dimensional concepts of typography. Perhaps the most important of these is the baseline—the imaginary line upon which most alphabet characters appear to sit. Although it is invisible, the baseline is the frame of reference for virtually all vertical measurements in typography. Leading, for example, is always expressed in baseline-to-baseline measurements. Nevertheless, some microcomputer programs that claim to be capable of typesetting do not subscribe to this convention, and some do so inconsistently. Some software, for instance, conceives of each letter as existing in an invisible but discretely bounded box, and placement of type is based on the boundaries of the boxes, not on the line of type's baseline.

This approach has two serious disadvantages. First, this method of reckoning is not consistent with standard approaches to typography, which means that your system will not be able to communicate effectively with commercial systems, which predominate in the market. Second, when you are looking at the page, it is not possible to tell where the boundaries of those boxes are, so measuring from one character to another does not necessarily tell you what the type specifications are. When measuring from the baseline, there is always a visible reckoning point from which to measure and calculate.

The baseline is crossed by the descenders of letters like y and p and also to a far lesser degree by round-bottomed characters like o and u. The reason for the latter is strictly visual. If the tapering curve of round-bottomed letters did not sink slightly below the baseline, they would appear to be floating above it. Round-topped letters get a treatment similar to round-bottomed ones. If an o were to sit precisely on the baseline and be precisely the same height as an x, it would appear too small relative to the other lowercase letters.

The *x-height* is a rough measure of lowercase letter height (which varies as a proportion of cap height—the height of the capital letters—from typeface to typeface). The x-height of a typeface is what its name indicates, the height of a lowercase x.

Cap height varies from face to face as well. Usually a typeface's cap height and the height of its ascenders are very close to equal, but in some common faces, such as Futura, the ascenders are taller. This has the general effect of making the lowercase letters look larger.

Of the design details of alphabetic characters, one of the most important is the *serif*, the small counterstrokes at the ends of a character's main strokes. Although serifs make a great contribution to typographic aesthetics, they are not fundamentally decorative. Serifs are signposts for the eye. By running at counter angles to the predominantly vertical strokes that make up Western letters, they

Antique Olive
ABCDEFGHIJKLMNOPQRSTUVWXYZ
abcdefghijklmnopqrstuvwxyz1234567890

Eras Book
ABCDEFGHIJKLMNOPQRSTUVWXYZ
abcdefghijklmnopqrstuvwxyz1234567890

Eurostile
ABCDEFGHIJKLMNOPQRSTUVWXYZ
abcdefghijklmnopqrstuvwxyz1234567890

Futura Book
ABCDEFGHIJKLMNOPQRSTUVWXYZ
abcdefghijklmnopqrstuvwxyz1234567890

Gill Sans
ABCDEFGHIJKLMNOPQRSTUVWXYZ
abcdefghijklmnopqrstuvwxyz1234567890

Helvetica
ABCDEFGHIJKLMNOPQRSTUVWXYZ
abcdefghijklmnopqrstuvwxyz1234567890

Optima
ABCDEFGHIJKLMNOPQRSTUVWXYZ
abcdefghijklmnopqrstuvwxyz1234567890

Figure 6-6 These text-weight sans serif faces illustrates several strategies for maintaining legibility in the absence of serifs. Antique Olive uses a very large x-height to facilitate recognition of the lowercase letters, while Optima uses subtle variations in stroke width, widening the strokes at the ends to suggest the presence of serifs.

provide a chance for the eye to orient itself, to see the trees despite the forest, so reading is easier.

The diversity among typefaces is amazing, especially considering the basic design constraints imposed by the letters themselves. Thousands of typefaces are available—and those are only the ones that are still in vogue. Because of their strong design component, typefaces are as prone to fashion fads as clothing styles, and the designs that can stand the test of time are rare. Of the thousands now in existence, only a handful adhere closely to pre-twentieth-century designs, although many are based on historical models.

Typefaces can be categorized in a number of ways. The fundamental divisions are *serif* and *sans serif; roman* and *italic;* and *typeface families.* Understanding the association between form and function within these divisions will help you make wise decisions when selecting and using typefaces for specific applications.

Serif vs. Sans Serif

Until the late-nineteenth century nearly all common typefaces were designed with serifs; because of the reading ease they offer, serif faces are still almost universally favored for book and periodical text. With the advent of the machine age, though, design tendencies favored a clean, machined look and sans serif (from the French, meaning "without serif") faces gained popularity. The movement toward sans serif faces reached its apex at the Bauhaus, the renowned German design school that was so influential in the 1920's and '30's (see Figure 6-6). Today, sans serif faces are a mainstay of popular and corporate typographic design.

In sans serif typefaces the strokes of the letters are usually of nearly even thicknesses, which tends to give them a very austere, mechanical appearance. This even, machined look, however, works against sans serif faces when they are used in text applications. Their uniform strokes tend to melt before the eye into a morass of like lines, and the more cap height vertical strokes there are, the harder the text is to read. Without the serifs' help in sorting out the strokes, the eye and brain need to work harder to decipher the marks. For proofreaders, mistakes become more difficult to detect.

For these reasons, sans serif typefaces are most useful in large point sizes—in newspaper headlines, book titles, advertisements, and chapter headings—or in small bursts that are designed to contrast with surrounding serif type. Sans serif type is typically used for signs—the simplicity of its letterforms and its untapering, uniform strokes make it readable at a distance. These same assertive characteristics make it useful for highlighting amid serif type, especially in listing, directory, and catalogue formats. And for those wanting the crisp, modern look of sans serif type with the readability afforded by serifs, a group of square-serif faces have evolved that take a sans serif approach to even letter-stroke weight, but deliver improved

Glypha 55
ABCDEFGHIJKLMNOPQRSTUVWXYZ
abcdefghijklmnopqrstuvwxyz1234567890

Lubalin Graph Book
ABCDEFGHIJKLMNOPQRSTUVWXYZ
abcdefghijklmnopqrstuvwxyz1234567890

Memphis Medium
ABCDEFGHIJKLMNOPQRSTUVWXYZ
abcdefghijklmnopqrstuvwxyz1234567890

Serifa 55
ABCDEFGHIJKLMNOPQRSTUVWXYZ
abcdefghijklmnopqrstuvwxyz1234567890

Figure 6-7 *Like the sans serif faces, square serif typefaces tend to feature wide characters and even stoke thicknesses. The serifs allow the lowercase letters to be shorter, proportioned more like classic serif faces.*

readability by terminating those strokes with crisply machined rectangular serifs (see Figure 6-7).

Roman vs. Italic

Another fundamental division among typefaces is based on radically divergent approaches to the styling of the letterforms themselves: roman vs. italic. Roman characters are upright letterforms, such as those used for this text, while italic characters are inclined to the right, in emulation of calligraphic, pen-drawn characters. When handwritten and calligraphic manuscripts were common, italic types were used as text faces, but nowadays they have been relegated to a role as a typographic device to create emphasis or to create contrast from surrounding roman text. Nearly every italic typeface is linked as a complement to a roman face; the two are designed to be used in conjunction to blend harmoniously on the page while still providing stylistic contrast.

Bodoni roman

Bodoni oblique

Bodoni italic

Figure 6-8 An oblique typeface is closely modeled after its parent roman face, although professionally designed obliques are specifically proportioned to accommodate the characters' rightward slant. The Bodoni oblique here has been electronically slanted by a computer. True Bodoni italic, designed with distinctly different letter shapes appears at bottom.

A typical use of italic type is to distinguish voices in written matter, as in a question-and-answer-style interview. Similarly, introductory passages are often placed in italic because they speak with a voice (often the editor's) that is separate from the text that follows.

Other common uses include distinguishing foreign words and phrases (The author described the political *zeitgeist* of the era); to distinguish a word being spoken of as an object (The word *there* is an overused expletive); and to create a visual representation of spoken inflection (She had the nerve to say *my* work was bad!). Because most italic faces are less legible than their roman counterparts, it is wise to keep italic passages short and to limit their use to a functional minimum. An entire page of italic matter can be a chore to read.

Although most typefaces have an italic complement, for design reasons or accidents of history many do not. The typographic need for italic complements gave rise to *oblique fonts*, which are basically versions of the roman fonts simply inclined to the right, in imitation of true italic fonts.

The semantics of the italic/oblique distinction can get a bit hazy. In practical parlance, the terms *oblique* and *italic* are often used interchangeably. Only by referring to a type sample book can you know which typefaces are true italics and which are actually obliqued versions of the roman faces. Muddying the waters further are typesetting systems that can electronically oblique fonts. Oblique fonts created by

Helvetica Lite

Helvetica Lite Italic

Helvetica

Helvetica Bold

Helvetica Heavy

Helvetica Black

Helvetica Black Italic

Helvetica Condensed

Helvetica Bold Condensed Italic

Helvetica Black Condensed

Helvetica Extended

Helvetica Black Extended

Helvetica Ultra Compressed

Helvetica Inserat

Helvetica Round Bold

__Figure 6-9__ The complete Helvetica family contains over 30 faces, some of which are illustrated here. The range of designs is achieved through variations in stroke weight, character width, and character slant. Although the inclined members of the Helvetica family are called italics, they are, in truth, obliques.

manufacturers of professional-quality fonts are typically not simple electronic obliques—they have been redrawn and redesigned as unique typefaces. Electronically obliqued fonts often suffer from distortions due to the methods used by the computer to create the slanted look—the formula the computer uses cannot take into account the myriad design decisions necessary.

Helvetica is one popular typeface that uses oblique rather than italic complements. The uniform thickness of the strokes of Helvetica letters (and the modernist tradition which gave rise to its design) make it incompatible with a calligraphic-style, true italic complementary face (see Figure 6-8).

Typeface Families

The fundamental division among typefaces is the family. A family of typefaces is bound together by a set of design concepts that allows the family members to be used in conjunction harmoniously.

By varying several parameters, type designers can create an extended family of related typefaces. The two most common of these variables are character width and stroke weight, and the names of the typefaces reflect these variables.

A typeface whose character widths have been narrowed is referred to as *condensed* or *compressed*. Those whose characters have been widened are said to be *expanded* or *extended*. For good measure, some families have members that are extra condensed, but because Western characters are based predominantly on vertical strokes, extra extended typefaces are rare. Because the eye relies for character identification on the relationships between vertical strokes, the increased character width drastically curtails legibility by separating the verticals and obscuring their interrelationships. As with obliquing, condensing and extending typefaces can also be done electronically, but again, proportioning and distortion problems arise that mandate redesign for professional-quality results.

Type families generally contain faces that express a range of varying weight, from lightness at one end of the spectrum to boldness at the other. Somewhere in the middle of this continuum, there is typically one face of median weight whose name is simply that of the family. Figure 6-9 shows members of the Helvetica family. At the middle of the pack there is simple Helvetica. Because of the multitude of Helvetica variants, Helvetica is often called Helvetica Regular. In a large minority of type families, though, there is no such generically named member. There is no such thing, for example, as plain old Futura. Each face has a specified weight: Futura Light, Book, Medium, and Bold (among others).

Naming schemes for typefaces are not standardized; there is no consensus on how "light" or how "bold" a character must be to earn those labels. Likewise, there is no agreement about how narrowed a face needs to be to rate the label of condensed or extra condensed. This is one of the reasons that a type sample book is a necessary tool for the typographer and designer.

Univers 45 (Lite)
ABCDEFGHIJKLMNOPQRSTUVWXYZ
abcdefghijklmnopqrstuvwxyz1234567890

Univers 56 (Italic)
ABCDEFGHIJKLMNOPQRSTUVWXYZ
abcdefghijklmnopqrstuvwxyz1234567890

Univers 67 (Bold Condensed)
ABCDEFGHIJKLMNOPQRSTUVWXYZ
abcdefghijklmnopqrstuvwxyz1234567890

Figure 6-10 Members of the Univers family are identified by number, although in type sample books they are also identified by traditional names, which refer literally to their weight and width.

There are a few type families that are organized under a numeric naming system, and the logic of the system is a relief from the general muddle of typographic conventions. These faces—including the Univers, Frutiger, and Glypha families—use a standard set of two-digit numbers to indicate their relationship to other family members. The first digit represents relative stroke weight: 4 = light, 5 = regular or book, 6 = bold, and 7 = extra bold. The second digit represents character width and oblique/italic status: 3 = extended roman, 4 = extended oblique/italic 5 = normal roman, 6 = normal italic, 7 = condensed roman, and 8 = condensed italic. Thus Univers 67 is bold condensed roman, and Frutiger 46 is light italic (see Figure 6-10). Such a logical approach is very atypical, however, in the tradition-based field of typography.

Another complication in describing typefaces arises from the absence of any authority that controls the naming and design of typefaces. Although there are thousands of professional-quality fonts available for commercial computerized typography, perhaps only about 2000 could be loosely described as "originals." Due to the inadequacy of the copyright laws as regards designs, typeface piracy—or more politely, design borrowing—has been a fact of the craft for centuries. Once the sincerest form of flattery, it has in the last fifty years become the sincerest form of capitalism. Every typeface manufacturer, for example, has some version of Helvetica, but that name is a registered trademark of the Linotype Corporation. In fact, Helvetica is derived from a nineteenth-century typeface, Akzidenz Grotesque. Typeface names can be trademarked, but designs have been nearly impossible to protect.

Elements of Styles

The design of typefaces is more that just functional and aesthetic—typefaces have emotive qualities and can exert powerful subliminal influences on the reader. Typefaces can evoke moods, from scholarly to whimsical, from urbane to strident, from nostalgic to visionary. These evocative capacities are an important element in the overall design equation of your publication, and the correct choice of typeface can heavily influence the effectiveness of printed matter. The arena in which this is most apparent is advertising typography, where competition for the eye is acute, where type can become associated with the product itself, and where the brevity of the message places a burden on the typography to carry a significant portion of the meaning.

The range of typeface choices for a designer can be staggering. The popular Mergenthaler font library, for instance, contains some 1800 typefaces, with more added monthly. This confusing array of choices can be tamed somewhat by organizing those typefaces into several categories and using the general characteristics of each as guidelines for the typefaces' effective use.

Typefaces can be split into three categories according to use: text, display, and decorative. Text faces, as the name implies, are used for lengthy passages of running text, as in a book or magazine. These faces place a great premium on legibility, especially in small point sizes. Their designs make it easy for the eye to scan quickly and effortlessly across lines of text, allowing for the easy recognition of all letters and words.

Display faces are designed for short passages of eye-arresting type, as in headlines, billboards, book and magazine covers, and signs. The letters of display faces can be more bold, extreme, or dramatic than those of text faces, and cause their primary function is to attract the eye, readability is not a major concern.

Decorative face designs are overtly evocative, and their letters may be customized almost to the point of illegibility. These fanciful faces are commonly used when a nontypeset look is desired. Popular decorative faces include script (popular for wedding invitations) and brush faces, which look hand-painted.

Text Faces

As a rule, text faces have serifs for ease of reading. Their tapering strokes are generally rather light, which allows their characters to sit in stark contrast to a white background. This lightness also serves to keep an all-text page from appearing too

Baskerville
ABCDEFGHIJKLMNOPQRSTUVWXYZ
abcdefghijklmnopqrstuvwxyz1234567890

ITC Bookman Lite
ABCDEFGHIJKLMNOPQRSTUVWXYZ
abcdefghijklmnopqrstuvwxyz1234567890

Century Schoolbook
ABCDEFGHIJKLMNOPQRSTUVWXYZ
abcdefghijklmnopqrstuvwxyz1234567890

ITC Cheltenham Book
ABCDEFGHIJKLMNOPQRSTUVWXYZ
abcdefghijklmnopqrstuvwxyz1234567890

ITC Garamond Book
ABCDEFGHIJKLMNOPQRSTUVWXYZ
abcdefghijklmnopqrstuvwxyz1234567890

Goudy Old Style
ABCDEFGHIJKLMNOPQRSTUVWXYZ
abcdefghijklmnopqrstuvwxyz1234567890

Times Roman
ABCDEFGHIJKLMNOPQRSTUVWXYZ
abcdefghijklmnopqrstuvwxyz1234567890

Figure 6-11 *Although many of the most popular text faces are based on centuries-old designs, most have been redesigned somewhat to reflect modern tastes. The faces shown here are among the most commonly used typefaces for books and magazines.*

dark, impenetrable, and uninviting. Some of the most popular text faces are shown in Figure 6-11.

Despite the serif faces' readability edge, sans serif faces, especially Helvetica, are often used for text. (Helvetica is one of the most legible and readable sans serif faces.) Apart from the readability problems posed by sans serif type, other problems arise with using sans serif faces for text. Because the strokes that make up sans serif characters are usually almost uniform in their thickness, there is very little variation in color over an entire page. The visual complexity afforded by tapered, serif characters is missing, and the page tends to take on a solid gray pallor—the text looks boring.

For related reasons, bold versions of serif faces should be avoided for long passages of running text; they are simply too wearisome on the eye. Like italics, bold faces are best reserved for emphasis or distinction.

The conservative, safe, and sensible approach, then, is to stick with serif faces when setting text. In the book community, this conservative approach almost always wins out, and books are seldom set in a sans serif typeface. When they are, line leading and letter spacing are usually very generous to break up the grayness and provide some relief for the eye. Running text is no place to experiment with exotic or alternative typefaces. An old book printer's adage advises, "When in doubt, use Caslon," a serif typeface designed over two hundred years ago. Designers may argue the pros and cons of Caslon, but few will argue about the logic of using conservative text faces.

Display Faces

Display faces are attention grabbers, used for headlines, cover type, titles, and chapter headings—short bursts of information where readability is assured by its position on the page, often with a lot of surrounding white space. They are also commonly used as visual punctuation to guide the eye around text pages that are set in directory or listing formats.

Display faces are usually distinguished by bold character strokes and distinctive designs, often with a blocky or architectural look. Because these faces are typically used in sizes much larger than typical text, their stroke weights tend to the extremes: some heavier for extra punch and some with a thinness that would severely hinder their readability at text sizes.

Text faces are often used as display faces, usually to take advantage of their textual connotations. Display type is recognized as a form of hype or exaggeration—associated with headlines, billboards, and howling newspaper ads. Text, by comparison, connotes factual representation. Hence text faces are often used in display roles to evoke an impression of factualness, verity, and honesty. The straightforward, sincere-sounding sales pitch will often be designed using a text-style face for its display type.

American Typewriter Medium
ABCDEFGHIJKLMNOPQRSTUVWXYZ
abcdefghijklmnopqrstuvwxyz1234567890

ITC Korinna
ABCDEFGHIJKLMNOPQRSTUVWXYZ
abcdefghijklmnopqrstuvwxyz1234567890

Italia Medium
ABCDEFGHIJKLMNOPQRSTUVWXYZ
abcdefghijklmnopqrstuvwxyz1234567890

Friz Quadrata
ABCDEFGHIJKLMNOPQRSTUVWXYZ
abcdefghijklmnopqrstuvwxyz1234567890

ITC Novarese Bold
ABCDEFGHIJKLMNOPQRSTUVWXYZ
abcdefghijklmnopqrstuvwxyz1234567890

ITC Serif Gothic Bold
ABCDEFGHIJKLMNOPQRSTUVWXYZ
abcdefghijklmnopqrstuvwxyz1234567890

ITC Souvenir Medium
ABCDEFGHIJKLMNOPQRSTUVWXYZ
abcdefghijklmnopqrstuvwxyz1234567890

Figure 6-12 Display faces vary widely in their versatility. American Typewriter, for example, is far more evocative than faces such as Italia and Souvenir, which limits their usefulness. The faces here are among the most popular for advertising typography.

Figure 6-13 *Decorative faces have limited applicability—they are designed for use in special situations. Their legibility is often compromised for their eye-catching qualities.*

Just making the letters large does not necessarily create effective display type, however. The issue is one of color—light and dark. If the characters are too light and delicate they will appear to float on the page, lacking impact. Because it is usually the dominant visual element of a layout, display type must anchor the page and help to unify all of the page's elements. Display faces are designed with the heft or character shapes to achieve this. Most bold sans serif faces and extra-bold serif faces can be used well in display roles.

Display faces are meant to divert the eye, so many liberties can be taken in their design. Nevertheless, some typefaces (as shown in Figure 6-12) are too parochial in their approach to be useful for widespread display use. An effective display face should be flexible and adaptable, and the typefaces in this figure assert themselves too strongly to be neutral. In general, it is preferable to have more well-rounded actors in your typographic repertory group.

Decorative Faces

In any type library, decorative faces are apt to be the least used. Decorative faces are to typography what a sand wedge is to golf—it isn't needed often, but when it is, nothing else will do. A graduation diploma set in Helvetica, for instance, would lose its character. In general, decorative faces are used where the typeface itself must bear a significant part of the narrative message.

Decorative faces are also often used as display type, but they tend to be too distinctive to blend well with the informational or text typefaces that usually accompany them. Decorative faces are often caricatures, specialists that can upstage accompanying text—they can be hard acts to follow. Figure 6-13 shows a selection of some of the more popular decorative typefaces.

Typefaces and Document Styles

There are no firm rules for mixing and matching faces on one page or within one document, but it is important to keep in mind that the interplay of typefaces is a function of the structure of the page. Typefaces should be selected as structural elements, not as decorative ones, to build documents, not adorn them.

Structurally, the gamut of type use can be divided into ad and poster work at one end of the spectrum and traditional book work at the other. In each case you must consider the degree of contrast that is desirable in the various typefaces and type sizes used. In a business or academic document, different typefaces are typically used to highlight chapter headings, section titles, subheads, and important text passages; in other words, their role is strictly functional, acting as visual guideposts to help the eye rapidly organize the pages. In such works, all the text is very tightly integrated, and the format of the document leads the eye from beginning to end. Excessive typographic diversity works against this overriding structural unity.

At the advertising end of the spectrum, the typefaces' role of linking elements is diminished as the decorative and dramatic functions increase in importance—variations in typeface are used to lure the eye around the page. Whereas Helvetica headers and Times text may make for stale-looking documents, a very large Helvetica headline and smaller Times text can function excellently in a poster or display ad.

The job at hand, then, determines how much liberty can be taken in mixing faces. In general, it's a wise policy to be fairly conservative about mixing faces in book and office document work. Typeface families are developed to allow typographic diversity while maintaining stylistic integrity. Take advantage of them.

When mixing type families within a document, a safe strategy is to assign typefaces according to the structural roles of the text elements and be consistent about this treatment. In this book, for instance, we use three levels of headings— main chapter headings and two levels of subordinate subheads. With the main chapter headings, we have our greatest typographic leeway, since these headings are designed predominantly as stand-alone elements, largely independent from the text. They dominate the design of the pages on which they appear.

The subheads, though, are bound with increasing tightness to the text within which they occur. The main subheads, set in 14-point Palatino Bold, denote major sections within the chapters. Their role is to interrupt and separate. They can wander slightly from the style of the text—their design needs to be graphically compatible, but there is some latitude for design divergence. The minor subheads—the most minor disruptions in the text flow—are designed for ease of text reference and represent no substantial break in the continuity of the text flow. At 10-point bold, they are most closely related to the style of the text.

The more integrated the roles of various text elements, the more important it is for them to be typographically compatible. *Headers* (like the chapter titles that run at the top of each page in this book) and *footers* (the page numbers at the bottoms of the pages), for example, are not integrally linked into the text of the page, so their typographic identities may derive from other parts of the book; a common design motif links the headers, the cover type, and the chapter titles.

Too many or disharmonious faces mixed on one page—or face changes that don't correlate to discrete functions within the page—can create a confused, carnival look that is visually distracting, creating an undesirable segmentation of the page. There are many ways to get a varied look on one page by creating variations in one type family using permutations of light/bold, roman/italic, uppercase/lowercase, big and small capitals, and character size. When in doubt, stick to one family as much as possible, reaching out to other families when added options are needed. And remember that typefaces are primarily structural elements. Their decorative role should be considered secondary.

Building a Font Library

One of the most important choices you'll make in setting up your desktop publishing system is what fonts to buy. No matter what kind of fonts your printer uses, buying fonts can cost a lot of money. For this reason, you need to buy fonts that are versatile, flexible, and middle-of-the-road. A good place to start is with a basic text family.

Times Roman or one of its many look-alikes is a logical place to start, if only because these faces are so popular. As with any text face, it is important to get the four basic family members: regular weight roman, regular weight italic, bold roman, and bold italic. If your system and your printer allow electronic obliquing, you can create a bold oblique and forego buying bold italic, but at least one true italic should be considered a necessity. Other yeoman text faces that should become increasingly popular and available for laser printers are Garamond, Century, Cheltenham, Caslon, Bembo, and Goudy. Considering the history of imitation in type design, the marketed versions of the faces may not bear these names, so compare their styles to the real things.

On the second shelf of your font library, you should put a versatile sans serif face with its bold complement. While Helvetica is a logical choice, like Times Roman it has become a typographic cliche. Although it's a good typeface, it pops up just about everywhere, and people are going to get tired of looking at it. For a more distinctive look, try members of the Avant Garde, Univers, or Gill Sans families. They too are fairly austere, but a bit more interesting. Another standby is Futura and its kissing cousin Spartan—both generic sans serif classics.

Restraint is advisable when selecting a face in the decorative category unless you know you are going to have a lot of use for it. Decorative faces are handy and attractive, but they tend to turn into white elephants after the novelty wears off. Finally, invest in a good pi font—one that contains most of the symbols you're apt to use: multiple-size bullets and ballot boxes, basic math symbols, copyright and trademark symbols, and maybe a star or two.

Chapter 7

Elements of Page Design

Electronic page makeup programs have helped to streamline the paste-up process by eliminating a lot of hand work. They also speed up the process of experimenting with varying page designs, because all changes can be handled electronically. These tools do little, however, to assist in making the design decisions that make pages work well and read well. This chapter will consider the rudiments of page design—some issues fundamental to making your pages work. We'll focus on structured documents—technical papers, newsletters, and reports—the formats most often used in business, educational, governmental, and traditional publishing applications.

Good design is above all functional, and the first task in designing pages is to determine what those pages need to accomplish. This starts with assessing the editorial content. From there, you can move to assembling the design elements used to present that information: headings, subheads, illustrations, captions, footnotes, and so on. The final task is integrating those elements harmoniously on the page.

Designing a Page Structure

Pages are not designed one at a time; they need a structure that will function for the whole job. For a newsletter, this basic page layout must be able to accommodate different article or department styles, as well as directories, illustrations, and advertisements. For an office document it must accommodate charts and tables, as well as pages on which the text is laid out with no graphic relief. In books it has to accommodate chapter headings, footnotes, bibliographies, and illustrations. Magazines need to accommodate all of the above plus sidebars and stories that open with introductory artwork.

The key to establishing page-to-page design consistency is creating a *page grid*—a background framework on which to hang editorial and graphic elements (see Figure 7-1). For traditional paste-up techniques, this grid is preprinted onto every paste-up board, giving the paste-up artist a complete set of horizontal and vertical alignment points for columns of type, headlines, illustrations, page numbers, footnotes, and other elements.

Electronic page makeup programs also have grid facilities, but they may not always be visible on screen. Highly interactive programs typically show the grid lines on screen, which allows the artist to accurately place page elements by eye. Other programs—such as those that paginate automatically—may instead have grid coordinates assigned in advance to the page elements, and once those elements have been identified, the program "pastes" them into their correct positions. In either case, the key to the system is the establishment of the grid that functions as the organizational map for each page.

One of the first problems the novice designer has is trying to do too much—trying to put too much on the page. In all events, avoid layout ad libbing—inventing ad hoc solutions can create a confused and unprofessional presentation. The best approach is to foresee your layout design needs and stick with a consistent plan.

Perhaps the single most important arbiter of page design for the laser publisher is page size. You will probably use the 8½-by-11-inch page size mandated by the laser printer itself. This is not, however, a very useful size for book work; it is more appropriate to magazine, journal, newsletter, and office jobs.

The main problem with this sheet size is column measure—the length of the typeset lines. Normal text type sizes of 10 or 11 points are simply too small to set in one column across a page this wide. Even with extra leading, the page will present itself as a gray slab, and readers will have difficulty following the lines of text as their eyes scan back from the left margin to the right. Using point sizes large enough to be proportionally appropriate to this large page (at least 12 points, and probably larger) is unsettling, because readers are not used to seeing commercial-style type set so large. You risk making the page look like a large-type publication for the visually impaired or a child's book. Furthermore, this solution is really a throwback to the look of the word-processed page, a look you are presumably trying to avoid.

Figure 7-1 (opposite) This sample page grid—based on the page design for a right-hand page in this book—lays out the major alignment points for text and graphic elements on the page. The baselines for each text line are indicated as well as alignment guides for folios and running heads.

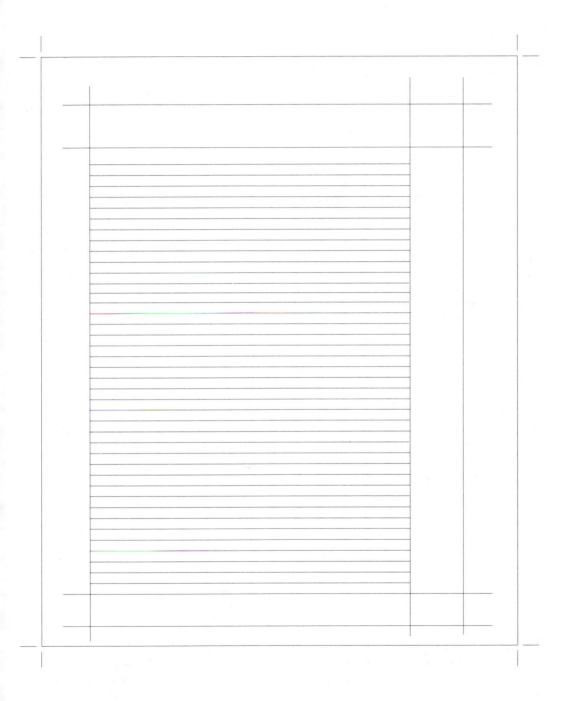

For some jobs it may be appropriate to create the pages on 8½-by-11-inch paper and then reduce the pages photographically to a more manageable format. In such cases, the text type should be set proportionately larger so that it will still be a readable size after reduction. A fringe benefit of this approach is that the reduction makes the type somewhat clearer by effectively reducing the dot size generated by the laser printer. Reducing a letter-size page by 25 percent gives a more book-like page size and gives 300-dpi type an appearance approximating 400-dpi type. On the negative side of the ledger is the extra cost of the photostating, which can make the use of laser typesetting less of a bargain.

Unillustrated Documents

In one regard, the unillustrated manuscript is the easiest to design, because it offers the fewest design options. In another way, however, it presents one of the most fundamental design challenges: the battle against gray. We have all picked up a book at some time, opened it, and when confronted with large pages of small type and narrow margins, have simply closed it and put it back on the shelf. Avoiding this formidable look is very important, especially in a page size as large as 8½ by 11. Examining the design of this most fundamental of pages is a good way to introduce some of the basic issues in any page design.

A page must present itself to the reader as a unified whole; all of the elements on a page must work together to give a cohesive appearance. This means you must establish a sense of visual balance, with no single element hogging all of the reader's attention. On the all-text page, this is not a great challenge, as competition for visual attention is scarce. The main competition is for the reader's attention.

The ally of the designer in pulling a page together is *negative space*—the white space on a page where there is no test or graphic image. This white space performs the dual tasks of keeping the page elements distinct from one another and providing a road map for the reader's eye, helping it to discern the flow of editorial traffic through the page. This is no less important on an all-text page than on an illustrated page.

The most common mistake in page design is trying to fit too much material on a page. Your sense of economy may tempt you to pack as much information on a page as you can, but the resulting density usually results in a muddled or impenetrable appearance. Even the eye needs breathing space. The problem for the all-text page is a scarcity of options for breaking up that gray.

One of the primary elements in page design is the outer margins. These margins are akin to a picture frame. In creating a page, you are creating a visual entity that must have distinct boundaries, and if you crowd the edges of the page, its contents threaten to push outward and off the page.

Because we read text horizontally, there is a visual flow along the left-right axis of a page, and the balance of left and right margins keeps the eye bouncing comfortably back and forth within the buffers of this space. Margins are like guard rails along a highway, and margins that are too narrow can allow the eye to careen right off the page.

There is a limit to how long a measure you can use to set lines of type and still expect the reader's eye to follow them sequentially without confusion. If you decide you need to set your pages in one-column format, you will have to pull in your left and right margins to bring line length down to a reasonable length. A 30- to 35-pica line length with 10-point type is pushing at the limits of practicality, but this can still leave 11-pica margins on the left and right—not an optimal solution, as there is as much horizontal white space as there is type. However, the narrower measure does make the page more readable (see Figure 7-2).

You may have noticed that the text in large-format, coffee-table art books is usually set very large. This is to beat the problem of wide column widths. Using 12-point type, you can extend line length by another 20 percent or so, to about 35 or 40 picas. Naturally, as line length increases, leading must also increase proportionately. For one-column pages, 2 points of extra lead per line should be considered a minimum.

A more satisfactory solution may be to use a multicolumn format. For all-text publications, it is wise to stop at two columns, even though this may create a look like that of an academic journal. At three columns, the pages begin to look like they're begging for illustrations, like those in familiar three-column magazine formats.

A two-column format allows you to use smaller text type, narrower column widths, and narrower margins. The addition of the gutter between the columns provides some added relief from the gray. Still, be generous with the left and right margins, and don't make the gutter too narrow—two picas is a workable mean (see Figure 7-3).

Another device for alleviating gray is using extra leading to indicate paragraph breaks, instead of the traditional first-line paragraph indents. For documents in which the paragraphs are short (less than 10 lines), half-line spaces may be sufficient. Documents with longer paragraphs may be able to take full line spaces between paragraphs without appearing too broken up and segmented. The

Figure 7-2 (following pages) The page on the left suffers from overcrowding. The insufficient margins not only make the page uninviting, they also make it difficult to read because the eye has a hard time finding its place when scanning from left margin to right. The page on the right not only has widened margins, but also has been set ragged right, and both changes enhance readability. Because the text area has been reduced, it seems to float somewhat on the page, and the ragged right margin makes the text area less stark and blocky. Like all the illustrations in this chapter, these pages are reduced from 8-1/2-by-11-inch format.

Greeking is a typographic term for type that is to be used for layout purposes only. Designers typically use greeking when they are creating comprehensive layouts—also called comps—for client approval. Because the type used for dummying pages or creating comps does not always need to be represent final copy, greeking is a fast, easy, and relatively inexpensive designer's tool.

Type shops usually have a file of greeked text on hand that they can run off quickly when a client requests it. Greeking plays a valuable role for the typographer as well, however. For years, typographers have used greeking that is specially written nonsense text—a long passage of "words" that reflect no true language—that presents in a reasonably concise form all of the common troublesome kerning pairs in the alphabet.

Because commercial typographic systems typically have kerning tables with over a thousand letter pairs, it is more expeditious to create greeked text that features all of these pairs than to hunt for them haphazardly in a passage of true text. When type shops refine their kerning pair values for a given typeface, they do so by running out their greeking files in that typeface and look for inadequately kerned letter combinations.

The term greeking, naturally, comes from the unintelligible appearance of such type, and harkens back to the words of the Shakespearean character who confessed that what he was hearing was all Greek to him.

With the advent of desktop laser printers, designers can now generate their own greeking, saving them a lot of time and money. Type shops, meanwhile, have lost a minor source of easy income. After all, setting greeking is about the easiest job a type shop ever gets. All they have to do is set the type in the right point size, column width, and typeface—the accuracy of the keystrokes is immaterial.

Greeking is a typographic term for type that is to be used for layout purposes only. Designers typically use greeking when they are creating comprehensive layouts—also called comps—for client approval. Because the type used for dummying pages or creating comps does not always need to be represent final copy, greeking is a fast, easy, and relatively inexpensive designer's tool.

Type shops usually have a file of greeked text on hand that they can run off quickly when a client requests it. Greeking plays a valuable role for the typographer as well, however. For years, typographers have used greeking that is specially written nonsense text—a long passage of "words" that reflect no true language—that presents in a reasonably concise form all of the common troublesome kerning pairs in the alphabet.

Because commercial typographic systems typically have kerning tables with over a thousand letter pairs, it is more expeditious to create greeked text that features all of these pairs than to hunt for them haphazardly in a passage of true text. When type shops refine their kerning pair values for a given typeface, they do so by running out their greeking files in that typeface and look for inadequately kerned letter combinations.

The term greeking, naturally, comes from the unintelligible appearance of such type, and harkens back to the words of the Shakespearean character who confessed that what he was hearing was all Greek to him.

With the advent of desktop laser printers, designers can now generate their own greeking, saving them a lot of time and money. Type shops, meanwhile, have lost a minor source of easy income. After all, setting greeking is about the easiest job a type shop ever gets. All they have to do is set the type in the right point size, column width, and typeface—the accuracy of the keystrokes is immaterial.

Greeking is a typographic term for type that is to be used for layout purposes only. Designers typically use greeking when they are creating comprehensive layouts—also called comps—for client approval. Because the type used for dummying pages or creating comps does not always need to be represent final copy, greeking is a fast, easy, and relatively inexpensive designer's tool.

Type shops usually have a file of greeked text on hand that they can run off quickly when a client requests it. Greeking plays a valuable role for the typographer as well, however. For years, typographers have used greeking that is specially written nonsense text—a long passage of "words" that reflect no true language—that presents in a reasonably concise form all of the common troublesome kerning pairs in the alphabet.

Because commercial typographic systems typically have kerning tables with over a thousand letter pairs, it is more expeditious to create greeked text that features all of these pairs than to hunt for them haphazardly in a passage of true text. When type shops refine their kerning pair values for a given typeface, they do so by running out their greeking files in that typeface and look for inadequately kerned letter combinations.

The term greeking, naturally, comes from the unintelligible appearance of such type, and harkens back to the words of the Shakespearean character who confessed that what he was hearing was all Greek to him.

With the advent of desktop laser printers, designers can now generate their own greeking, saving them a

Greeking is a typographic term for type that is to be used for layout purposes only. Designers typically use greeking when they are creating comprehensive layouts—also called comps—for client approval. Because the type used for dummying pages or creating comps does not always need to be represent final copy, greeking is a fast, easy, and relatively inexpensive designer's tool.

Type shops usually have a file of greeked text on hand that they can run off quickly when a client requests it. Greeking plays a valuable role for the typographer as well, however. For years, typographers have used greeking that is specially written nonsense text—a long passage of "words" that reflect no true language—that presents in a reasonably concise form all of the common troublesome kerning pairs in the alphabet.

Because commercial typographic systems typically have kerning tables with over a thousand letter pairs, it is more expeditious to create greeked text that features all of these pairs than to hunt for them haphazardly in a passage of true text. When type shops refine their kerning pair values for a given typeface, they do so by running out their greeking files in that typeface and look for inadequately kerned letter combinations.

The term greeking, naturally, comes from the unintelligible appearance of such type, and harkens back to the words of the Shakespearean character who confessed that what he was hearing was all Greek to him.

With the advent of desktop laser printers, designers can now generate their own greeking, saving them a lot of time and money. Type shops, meanwhile, have lost a minor source of easy income. After all, setting greeking is about the easiest job a type shop ever gets. All they have to do is set the type in the right point size, column width, and typeface—the accuracy of the keystrokes is immaterial.

Greeking is a typographic term for type that is to be used for layout purposes only. Designers typically use greeking when they are creating comprehensive layouts—also called comps—for client approval. Because the type used for dummying pages or creating comps does not always need to be represent final copy, greeking is a fast, easy, and relatively inexpensive designer's tool.

Type shops usually have a file of greeked text on hand that they can run off quickly when a client requests it. Greeking plays a valuable role for the typographer as well, however. For years, typographers have used greeking that is specially written nonsense text—a long passage of "words" that reflect no true language—that presents in a reasonably concise form all of the common troublesome kerning pairs in the alphabet.

Because commercial typographic systems typically have kerning tables with over a thousand letter pairs, it is more expeditious to create

Elements of Page Design

Greeking is a typographic term for type that is to be used for layout purposes only. Designers typically use greeking when they are creating comprehensive layouts—also called comps—for client approval. Because the type used for dummying pages or creating comps does not always need to be represent final copy, greeking is a fast, easy, and relatively inexpensive designer's tool.

Type shops usually have a file of greeked text on hand that they can run off quickly when a client requests it. Greeking plays a valuable role for the typographer as well, however. For years, typographers have used greeking that is specially written nonsense text—a long passage of "words" that reflect no true language—that presents in a reasonably concise form all of the common troublesome kerning pairs in the alphabet.

New Youth Center

Because commercial typographic systems typically have kerning tables with over a thousand letter pairs, it is more expeditious to create greeked text that features all of these pairs than to hunt for them haphazardly in a passage of true text. When type shops refine their kerning pair values for a given typeface, they do so by running out their greeking files in that typeface and look for inadequately kerned letter combinations.

The term greeking, naturally, comes from the unintelligible appearance of such type, and harkens back to the words of the Shakespearean character who confessed that what he was hearing was all Greek to him.

With the advent of desktop laser printers, designers can now generate their own greeking, saving them a lot of time and money. Type shops, meanwhile, have lost a minor source of easy income. After all, setting greeking is about the easiest job a type shop ever gets. All they have to do is set the type in the right point size, column width, and typeface—the accuracy of the keystrokes is immaterial.

the type used for dummying pages or creating comps does not always need to be represent final copy, greeking is a fast, easy, and relatively inexpensive designer's tool.

Type shops usually have a file of greeked text on hand that they can run off quickly when a client requests it. Greeking plays a valuable role for the typographer as well, however. For years, typographers have used greeking that is specially written nonsense text—a long passage of "words" that reflect no true language—that presents in a reasonably concise form all of the common troublesome kerning pairs in the alphabet.

Greeking is a typographic term for type that is to be used for layout purposes only. Designers typically use greeking when they are creating comprehensive layouts—also called comps—for client approval. Because the type used for dummying pages or creating comps does not always need to be represent final copy, greeking is a fast, easy, and relatively inexpensive designer's tool.

Type shops usually have a file of greeked text on hand that they can run off quickly when a client requests it. Greeking plays a valuable role for the typographer as well, however. For years, typographers have used greeking that is specially written nonsense text—a long passage of "words" that reflect no true language—that presents in a reasonably concise form all of the common troublesome kerning pairs in the alphabet.

Senior Citizen Activities

Because commercial typographic systems typically have kerning tables with over a thousand letter pairs, it is more expeditious to create greeked text that features all of these pairs than to hunt for them haphazardly in a passage of true text. When type shops refine their kerning pair values for a given typeface, they do so by running out their greeking files in that typeface. The term greeking, naturally, comes from the unintelligible appearance of such type, and harkens back to the words of the idea here is to add a little air to the page layout without fracturing the text into a lot of little gray squares.

A related device is the use of subheads within the text. These text headings are typically set in boldface in the same size as the body text. Subheads can bring a small measure of graphic diversity to the page. This is common in newspaper work, where subheads are peppered at fairly regular intervals throughout a story. They are typically used in association with line spaces, while the other paragraphs are demarcated by first-line indents. These small, bold call-outs are arguably functional editorial elements, allowing the reader to scan the progress of the article without having to read all the way through it. They can also provide transitions between sections of an article with an economy of words. Their main role, though, is often as design elements that prevent a long article from seeming so foreboding. They provide rest stations for the eye. You may have noticed that you are often more apt to read more pages of a book in one sitting if the book's chapters are relatively short. It is natural to read from one break point to the next. This same principle is at work in a newspaper's subheads. If they are placed at regular, short intervals, the readers are apt to keep reading longer.

Subheads, then, are very useful from both design and editorial perspectives. In this book, we have used two levels of subordinate subheads, organized like the levels of an outline. Our primary subheads divide the chapters into major subsections. Their importance is typographically signified by their size and prominence on the page. Secondary subheads have less graphic impact, relating to the level of division they represent within the organization of the book.

Top and Bottom Margins

The top and bottom of a page must serve as containment just like the left and right margins. The top of the page is arguably more important, because it's where the eye typically enters the page. It's a good idea to design your pages with firm top margins, curtain rods from which hang the banners that are your pages. This creates an organizing anchor for the page, and it keeps the elements of the page from seeming to drift upward and off the page. Whereas the gray rectangle of type in a single-column, wide-set page (as in a novel) creates its own page lid, a two-column format like the one described may tend to look like New York's World Trade Center, towering upward. Putting wider margins at the tops of the pages

Figure 7-3 *(opposite) Ragged right margins make sense in an unillustrated two-column layout, because they keep the layout from appearing too blocky. The graphic header with an ample top margin provides needed containment for the text. Paragraph breaks have been denoted with extra leading in order to add some breathing space to the page.*

(relative to the left and right margins) tempers this visual effect. Likewise, a simple graphic element such as a horizontal rule can neatly cap such a format.

Bottom margins are typically not identical to the top margins—a perfect symmetry between white space at the top and bottom of a page is not important, and usually not desirable because it makes the page appear very static. The difference between the top and bottom margins needs to be the equivalent of only a couple of text lines. The amount of extra space allotted depends in part on the presence of repetitive text or graphic elements that occur at the top of each page (headers) or at the bottom (footers). The presence of these elements might dictate more room (depending on their complexity and size) in the corresponding margin.

Although they may seem like minor adornments, headers and footers such as chapter titles and page numbers create a subtle form of punctuation on a page. Headers, which may be repetitions of chapter or section titles, provide a nice excuse for the graphic lids in the illustrations, even though they may not be editorially necessary. Likewise footers, including *folios* (more modestly known as page numbers), can provide a finishing trim for the bottom of the page. Because we read pages from side to side, left and right boundaries on a page manifest themselves almost automatically. Top and bottom boundaries are helped out by such small visual cues. They also assist the reader in locating a particular section when paging quickly through the document.

Another layout variation that can provide some editorial as well as graphic latitude is the *sidebar.* A sidebar is a self-contained editorial unit that sits within a main body of text. It's particularly popular in magazines and is often used in large feature newspaper articles as well. As an editorial device, it allows you to add a sidelight to the main text without an elaborate transition or digression within the main text. Graphically, it allows you to add variety to a page by creating a contrasting visual entity on the page. A sales report set in a two-column format, for instance, can contain a series of client profiles set in a three-column format and surrounded by a ruled box. A sidebar should be viewed as a page within itself, with its own demands for breathing space afforded by white space margins and sufficient gutters (see Figure 7-4).

Text Specifications

The dimensions of the page and grid form the basis for your typographic decisions. Once you've established the format of the pages, you have to establish type

Figure 7-4 (opposite) *The sidebar at the bottom of this page provides both editorial and graphic flexibility. The box that contains the sidebar is set to the full width of the text above it, and the margins within the box mirror those of the whole page. The three-column format within the sidebar gives the page additional visual interest.*

12   *Talking Type*

■■■■■■■■■■■■■■■■■■■■■■■■■■■■■■

Greeking is a typographic term for type that is to be used for layout purposes only. Designers typically use greeking when they are creating comprehensive layouts—also called comps—for client approval. Because the type used for dummying pages or creating comps does not always need to be represent final copy, greeking is a fast, easy, and relatively inexpensive designer's tool.

Type shops usually have a file of greeked text on hand that they can run off quickly when a client requests it. Greeking plays a valuable role for the typographer as well, however. For years, typographers have used greeking that is specially written nonsense text—a long passage of "words" that reflect no true language—that presents in a reasonably concise form all of the common troublesome kerning pairs in the alphabet.

Because commercial typographic systems typically have kerning tables with over a thousand letter pairs, it is more expeditious to create greeked text that features all of these pairs than to hunt for them haphazardly in a passage of true text. When type shops

refine their kerning pair values for a given typeface, they do so by running out their greeking files in that typeface and look for inadequately kerned letter combinations.

Greeking is a typographic term for type that is to be used for layout purposes only. Designers typically use greeking when they are creating comprehensive layouts—also called comps—for client approval. Because the type used for dummying pages or creating comps does not always need to be represent final copy, greeking is a fast, easy, and relatively inexpensive designer's tool.

Type shops usually have a file of greeked text on hand that they can run off quickly when a client requests it. Greeking plays a valuable role for the typographer as well, however. For years, typographers have used greeking that is specially written nonsense text—a long passage of "words" that reflect no true language—that presents in a reasonably concise form all of the common troublesome kerning pairs in the alphabet. Because commercial typographic systems typically have kerning tables with over a thousand

Profile: Claude Garamond

With the advent of desktop laser printers, designers can now generate their own greeking, saving them a lot of time and money. Type shops, meanwhile, have lost a minor source of easy income. After all, setting greeking is about the easiest job a type shop ever gets. All they have to do is set the type in the right point size, column width, and typeface—the accuracy of the keystrokes is immaterial.

Greeking is a typographic term for type that is to be used for layout purposes only. Designers typically use greeking when they are creating comprehensive layouts, also called comps, for client approval. Because the type used for dummying pages or creat-

ing comps does not always need to be represent final copy, greeking is a fast, easy, and relatively inexpensive designer's tool.

Type shops usually have a file of greeked text on hand that they can run off quickly when a client requests it. Greeking plays a valuable role for the typographer as well, however.

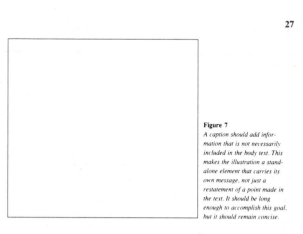

27

Figure 7
A caption should add information that is not necessarily included in the body text. This makes the illustration a stand-alone element that carries its own message, not just a restatement of a point made in the text. It should be long enough to accomplish this goal, but it should remain concise.

Greeking is a typographic term for type that is to be used for layout purposes only. Designers typically use greeking when they are creating comprehensive layouts—also called comps—for client approval. Because the type used for dummying pages or creating comps does not always need to be represent final copy, greeking is a fast, easy, and relatively inexpensive designer's tool.

Type shops usually have a file of greeked text on hand that they can run off quickly when a client requests it. Greeking plays a valuable role for the typographer as well, however. For years, typographers have used greeking that is specially written nonsense text—a long passage of "words" that reflect no true language—that presents in a reasonably concise form all of the common troublesome kerning pairs in the alphabet.

Next Year's Profit Picture

With the advent of desktop laser printers, designers can now generate their own greeking, saving them a lot of time and money. Type shops, meanwhile, have lost a minor source of easy income. After all, setting greeking is about the easiest job a type shop ever gets. All they have to do is set the type in the right point size, column width, and typeface—the accuracy of the keystrokes is immaterial.

Because commercial typographic systems typically have kerning tables with over a thousand letter pairs, it is more expeditious to create greeked text that features all of these pairs than to hunt for them haphazardly in a passage of true text. When type shops refine their kerning pair values for a given typeface, they do so by running out their greeking files in that typeface and specifications for the text. This will depend in large part on the typographic capabilities of the typesetting program you use.

Your first decision should focus on column margin treatment. Your basic choices here are justified or ragged right. A ragged right configuration is another way to alleviate gray, slab-like text, and it also reduces problems that can arise from weak hyphenation programs. A typesetting program with modest hyphenation abilities may force unacceptable stretching of spacebands to accomplish justification. Because consistent type color is important for the readability and appearance of a page, you want to limit the amount of variation in word and letterspacing in your text. If your typesetting program has difficulties in creating an even type color, a ragged right set will enhance the appearance of the pages.

The type size you choose depends on your selected column width. In general, try to stick with 11-point or 12-point type. Some publications may require slightly larger body type, but smaller sizes should be reserved for multicolumn formats and small passages of text, as in footnotes and captions.

Paragraph indention should relate to column width. Paragraph indents are important visual cues, and they must be deep enough to stand out against the column width. One-em indents are sufficient for narrow columns of up to about 12 to 15 picas. After that, they can be deeper. In wide columns, they can be very deep—four ems and more. Keep their function in mind: they are visual punctuation, so make them large enough to stand out, but not so large as to be disruptive. If you are using added leading to break your paragraphs, first-line indents are probably unnecessary and may look awkward.

Using Illustrations

Adding illustrations to your document not only adds another avenue of communication, it also opens up your page layouts and makes them more interesting. Although you may be able to express information perfectly well in prose form, a table, chart, or graph can have more impact on the reader and act as a landmark in the text when the reader is searching for specific information.

Single-Column Formats In illustrating the single-column page, your best bet is simplicity, pushing the illustrations to the top of the page or the bottom. Figure 7-5 shows one approach to this, demonstrating how you can accommodate the shape

Figure 7-5 (opposite) Caption placement can be modified to accommodate illustrations of varying shapes. A square or vertical illustration can be captioned at the side to keep the illustration in proportion to the page. Horizontal illustrations can be used at full text-column width with captions placed below them in the traditional manner.

of your illustration by varying the placement of the caption. This design allows for an alternate illustration width in addition to one that spans the entire text column. In the illustration, the picture was given the narrow treatment, because if it were allowed to span the whole text column, it would take over the entire page. A horizontal picture, on the other hand, can be used at full width and still stay in proportion to the text area.

In some cases, you can run illustrations in the middle of a one-column page, but these need to be handled with care. Such figures should be kept fairly shallow, because they threaten to segment the page into a stack of boxes, an undesirable design effect called *tombstoning*. If you plan to run such an illustration in the middle of page, avoid setting it within a ruled box, as the box exaggerates the tombstone effect.

When deciding whether an illustration should go at the bottom or top of the page, consider its height. As a general rule, if it's less than a third of a page deep, it should go at the top. If it's deeper than that, you have the option of top or bottom placement. Consider the placement in terms of the illustrations' buoyancy—larger or heavier ones should be allowed to sink to the bottom of the page, and light, airy, or small ones should float to the top. Once the illustration exceeds two thirds of a page deep, it should probably get a page of its own, because any text on such a page will tend to get overshadowed.

Shaping your text around an illustration is a tempting design option, but in practice, it is usually more work than it's worth, and although it may seem fancy, in truth it doesn't do very much to enhance the look of a page and may actually hinder the readability of the text.

Two-Column Formats   Handling illustrations in a two-column format is little different than in one-column format, especially if the pages are sparsely illustrated. Letting the illustrations straddle the two columns creates the most forceful presentation. In a heavily illustrated two-column document, you can also add single-column illustrations to provide a measure of design diversity, but if your illustrations are few in number, these small pictures lack the punch needed to liven up your pages.

In two-column pages, page-wide illustrations in the middle of the page should be avoided. They unnecessarily segment the page and create a confused layout. This effect arises because text set in two columns does not have the graphic strength on the page that a single, wide column of text has—the text lacks the bulk necessary to balance the weight of the illustration.

Figure 7-6 *(opposite) In this illustration, the text columns are not centered on the page, and to maintain a sense of visual balance, the caption has been placed in a third, smaller column. When straddling text columns with illustrations, make sure there is enough text to support the weight of the illustration.*

Greeking is a typographic term for type that is to be used for layout purposes only. Designers typically use greeking when they are creating comprehensive layouts—also called comps—for client approval. Because the type used for dummying pages or creating comps does not always need to be represent final copy, greeking is a fast, easy, and relatively inexpensive designer's tool.

Type shops usually have a file of greeked text on hand that they can run off quickly when a client requests it. Greeking plays a valuable role for the typographer as well, however. For years, typographers have used greeking that is specially written nonsense text—a long passage of "words" that reflect no true language—that presents in a reasonably concise form all of the common troublesome kerning pairs in the alphabet.

Because commercial typographic systems typically have kerning tables with over a thousand letter pairs, it is more expeditious to create greeked text that features all of these pairs than to hunt for them haphazardly in a passage of true text. When type shops refine their kerning pair values for a given typeface, they do so by running out their greeking files in that typeface and look for inadequately kerned letter combinations.

The term greeking, naturally, comes from the unintelligible appearance of such type, and harkens back to the words of the Shakespearean character who confessed that what he was hearing was all Greek to him.

With the advent of desktop laser printers, designers can now generate their own greeking, saving them a lot of time and money. Type shops, meanwhile, have lost a minor source of easy income. After all, setting greeking is about the easiest job a type shop ever gets. All they have to do is set the type in the right point size, column width, and typeface—the accuracy of the keystrokes is immaterial.

Figure 7
A caption should add information that is not necessarily included in the body text. This makes the illustration a standalone element that carries its own message, not just a restatement of point made in the text. It should be long enough to accomplish this goal, but it should remain concise.

A fresh group of temporary workers got hearty greetings from the 2nd shift workers at the recently too-busy Hornwood rendering plant.

Temporary Workers Give Relief to Overworked 2nd Shift in Hornwood Plant

Greeking is a typographic term for type that is to be used for layout purposes only. Designers typically use greeking when they are creating comprehensive layouts—also called comps—for client approval. Because the type used for dummying pages or creating comps does not always need to be represent final copy, greeking is a fast, easy, and relatively inexpensive designer's tool.

Type shops usually have a file of greeked text on hand that they can run off quickly when a client requests it. Greeking plays a valuable role for the typographer as well, however. For years, typographers have used greeking that is specially written nonsense text—a long passage of "words" that reflect no true language—that presents in a reasonably concise form all of the common troublesome kerning pairs in the alphabet.

Because commercial typographic systems typically have kerning tables with over a thousand letter pairs, it is more expeditious to create greeked text that features all of these pairs than to hunt for them haphazardly in a passage of true text. When type shops refine their kerning pair values for a given typeface, they do so by running out their greeking files in that typeface and look for inadequately kerned letter combinations.

The term greeking, naturally, comes from the unintelligible appearance of such type, and harkens back to the words of the Shakespearean character who confessed that what he was hearing was all Greek to him.

With the advent of desktop laser printers, designers can now generate their own greeking, saving them a lot of time and money. Type shops, meanwhile, have lost a minor source of easy income. After all, setting greeking is about the easiest job a type shop ever gets. All they have to do is set the type in the right point size, column width, and typeface—the accuracy of the keystrokes is immaterial.

Greeking is a typographic term for type that is to be used for layout purposes only. Designers typically use

Continued on Page 9

Bosworth Named V.P. of Sales for Southwest

Greeking is a typographic term for type that is to be used for layout purposes only. Designers typically use greeking when they are creating comprehensive layouts—also called comps—for client approval. Because the type used for dummying pages or creating comps does not always need to be represent final copy, greeking is a fast, easy, and relatively inexpensive designer's tool.

Type shops usually have a file of greeked text on hand that they can run off quickly when a client requests it. Greeking plays a valuable role for the typographer as well, however. For years, typographers have used greeking that is specially written nonsense text—a long passage of "words" that

T.R. "Pinky" Bosworth, new Vice President of Sales

"words" that reflect no true language— that presents in a reasonably concise form all of the common troublesome kerning pairs in the alphabet.

Because commercial typographic systems typically have kerning tables with over a thousand letter pairs, it is more expeditious to create greeked text that features all of these pairs than to hunt for them haphazardly in a passage of true text.

6

For this same reason, page-wide illustrations in two-column formats look better at the top of the page than at the bottom. As seen in Figure 7-6, the columns of text beneath the photograph act in an architectural way, supporting the picture and holding it aloft. Text columns set above such an illustration have to be large enough to keep the page from looking bottom-heavy.

Three-Column Formats   The three-column format offers the most design options, and this makes it very popular for magazine and newsletter work. It also makes it the most rigorous kind of page to design. As noted earlier, this format begs for illustrations, so it should be used only when you have a lot of graphics to add to your pages and the time to make numerous design decisions. On those pages that lack illustrations, you'll need to add typographic devices, such as rules, background screens, and point size and typeface changes to add visual diversity. It's also important to spread the illustrations evenly throughout the document, to maintain an even level of design complexity (see Figure 7-7).

The three-column format gives you the option of placing your illustrations across one, two, or three columns. In the last case, dividing the page into upper and lower halves allows you to place illustrations without having to worry about alignment over the text columns, as in Figure 7-8.

The key to making a three-column format work is taking advantage of the many options available to you. At the outset, a wise course of action is to design a set of six or eight "master pages" templates you can use as page models. In these pages, you can outline your basic options for handling text and graphics. Referring to these archetypes will save you a lot of time-consuming case-by-case design decisions later.

The importance of establishing a comprehensive page grid is most dramatically evidenced in working with three-column pages. Having a visible and well-thought-out grid can make many design decisions much simpler by allowing you to run through different designs by simply following the predrawn options offered by the lines of the grid. This process of testing for workable layouts is called *dummying,* and having the skeleton of the page preestablished allows you to make up dummy pages much faster and makes your design options more apparent.

Creating page-design templates has the added advantage of freeing the designer from many of the more routine page makeup tasks, with these templates acting like menus in a design cookbook. You can also purchase sets of predesigned

Figure 7-7 (opposite) Illustrations in three-column formats must provide movement in the layout to keep it from becoming static. Here, the illustrations create a graphic axis from upper left to lower right, while the display type creates a counter-movement from upper right to lower left. These simple layout dynamics are very important in keeping three-column formats lively.

Harold Welmsley (English, 1881-1962)—"An Outing in Wiffordshire," drypoint and aquatint, with hand coloring

Katarina Higmunds-Getzfurlichkeitzen (German, b. 1923)—"Die Mausgeschifte," oil on canvas, with sticks, string, sand, human hair, and newspaper

Greeking is a typographic term for type that is to be used for layout purposes only. Designers typically use greeking when they are creating comprehensive layouts—also called comps—for client approval. Because the type used for dummying pages or creating comps does not always need to be represent final copy, greeking is a fast, easy, and relatively inexpensive designer's tool.

Type shops usually have a file of greeked text on hand that they can run off quickly when a client requests it. Greeking plays a valuable role for the typographer as well, however. For years, typographers have used greeking that is specially written nonsense text—a long passage of "words" that reflect no true language—that presents in a reasonably concise form all of the common troublesome kerning pairs in the alphabet.

Because most popular commercial typographic systems typically have kerning tables with over a thousand letter pairs, it is more expeditious to create greeked text that features all of these pairs than to hunt for them haphazardly in a passage of true text. When type shops refine their kerning pair values for a given typeface, they do so by running out their greeking files in that typeface and look for inadequately kerned letter combinations.

The term greeking, naturally, comes from the unintelligible appearance of such type, and harkens back to the words of the Shakespearean character who confessed that what he was hearing was all Greek to him.

With the advent of desktop laser printers, designers can now generate their own greeking, saving them a lot of time and money. Type shops, meanwhile, have lost a minor source of easy income. After all, setting greeking is about the easiest job a type shop ever gets. All they have to do is set the type in the right point size, column width, and typeface—the accuracy of the keystrokes is immaterial.

Greeking is a typographic term for type that is to be used for layout purposes only. Designers typically use greeking when they are creating comprehensive layouts–called comps–for client approval. Because the type used for dummying pages or creating comps does not always need to be represent final copy, greeking is a fast, easy, and relatively inexpensive designer's tool.

Type shops usually have a file of greeked text on hand that they can run off quickly when a client requests it. Greeking plays a valuable role for the typographer as well, however. For years, typographers have used greeking that is specially written nonsense text (a long passage of "words" that reflect no true language) that presents in a reasonably concise form all of the common troublesome kerning pairs in the alphabet.

Commercial typographic systems typically have kerning tables with over a thousand letter pairs, so it is more expeditious to create greeked text that features all of these pairs than to hunt for them haphazardly in a passage of templates made specifically for many of the page makeup programs now on the market. These templates can get you up and running very quickly if you are unsure of your own design prowess or simply don't have the time to spend designing all your pages. They can also act as excellent starting points for your own custom designs.

Getting Help

Because the appearance of a document is central to its editorial effectiveness, it's important for you to make a serious investment in your publications' designs. Although desktop publishing is based largely on a do-it-yourself ethic, we highly recommend that you enlist the counsel of a skilled designer in getting your publications off on the right foot.

In addition, it's important to arm yourself with some basic design reference texts, a list of which are included in the bibliography at the end of this book. Perhaps the best thing you can do for the design of your document, though, is to shop around. Look closely at other document designs on the newsstand and in the library. Your final design decisions must be a synthesis derived from the demands of your publications' content and the way you want to present it.

Figure 7-8 (opposite) On this page, the illustrations straddle the text columns, but do not align with the text's margins—the horizontal strength of the illustrations' arrangement make this unnecessary. The gutter rules between the text columns aid the readability of the justified columns, but they would be distracting between columns of ragged-right type.

Chapter 8

The Machinery of Desktop Publishing

In the nineteenth century, a French school of painting called pointillism enjoyed a brief period of popularity. Renouncing the use of brush strokes to render their landscapes, the pointillist painters instead used tiny dots of color. When viewed close up, their paintings resembled mosaics, but from a suitable distance the individual dots merged to form coherent images.

The term *raster imaging* was originally coined to describe the scan lines used by televisions and other video machines. Eventually, it came to mean all technologies that, like pointillism, render images as patterns of tiny dots of uniform size, laid out on an invisible grid. It is the process that the laser printer uses to transfer images to paper. Each dot and each white spot in the image corresponds respectively to a bit, an electronic on-signal or off-signal. Hence the term *bit map* to describe the electronic pattern that matches the printed image. Considered in the abstract, the various steps of desktop publishing involve generating, manipulating, and printing bit maps.

This chapter looks at the three types of bit-map processing hardware that are used in desktop publishing: laser printers, which render both text and graphics as patterns of dots on paper; scanners or digitizers, which create digital bit maps from analog images such as photographs, hand-drawn images, or video signals; and personal computers, which run the software that links up the various parts of the publishing system.

Laser Printers

Very expensive laser printers have been used as high-speed line printers connected with mainframe computers since the mid-1970's, but it wasn't until 1984 that laser printers in the under-$10,000 range became available. The personal computer industry quickly embraced these machines as replacements for daisy-wheel printers, valuing their quiet, fast operation and their "high resolution" (300-dpi) output. Their reception by the publishing industry, in contrast, was somewhat cool. Previously, the low end of typesetting resolution had been 600 dpi, the resolution at which individual dots are no longer discernible. To the eye trained to appreciate quality in type, the output of a laser printer was definitely substandard—it was simply too coarse.

Whether your perspective is that of the personal computer user accustomed to squinting over faded dot matrix printouts or of the publishing professional used to silver-film galleys, the laser printer is the defining factor of desktop publishing. Actually, many types of "laser printers" use imaging mechanisms other than lasers; in this book we go along with the convention of using laser printer as a generic term for any sort of plain paper, raster-imaging printer with a resolution of 240 to 600 dpi. Higher resolution machines do play a role in desktop publishing. In particular, some phototypesetting machines are now equipped with page description languages that make them compatible with any lower resolution machine running the same language. This compatibility allows you to carry out all preliminary tasks on the laser printer and then use a high-quality phototypesetting machine for final output.

Xerography

The technology most commonly used by laser printers for transferring an image onto paper is *xerography*. This technique makes the laser printer a close cousin to the standard photocopying machine; in fact, the first inexpensive laser printers came about as a spinoff of research into digital photocopying machines. Costs plunged when manufacturers, led by Canon, found ways of adapting designs and even some parts from low-end photocopiers to laser printers.

In essence, xerography is a type of photography, in which the film is a drum coated with a material that picks up or disperses an electronic charge wherever it is exposed to light. In a photocopying machine, the image on the drum is formed by reflecting a bright light off the item resting on the glass plate. In most laser printers, the image to be printed is traced onto the drum by a laser beam or some other light source that turns on and off under the control of a computer. Some printers are "write white," meaning that they print the areas not activated by the imaging mechanism.

Once the electronic pattern is formed on the photosensitive drum, the next step is to transfer it to paper. As the drum turns, it picks up toner—in this case, very fine plastic particles carrying the opposite charge. Initially adhering to the drum, the particles are then pulled away by the paper. Heated rollers seal the toner onto the paper surface.

Due to the heat used to weld the image onto paper, xerographic printers are unsuitable for printing some types of label sheets, envelopes, or other materials with pressure-sensitive or heat-sensitive adhesives. On the other hand, such printers have the capability of printing on materials other than paper, including clear acetate for use in overhead projections.

As discussed earlier, the quality of laser-printed output depends primarily on the number of dots per inch in the image. Less obviously, though, it also depends on the shape and uniformity of the dots, which may be rectangles, squares, ovals, circles, or irregular blotches. If the printer produces very crisp dots, the jagged look of diagonal lines or diagonal strokes on characters may be more pronounced. If the dots tend to vary in size and wander slightly from their correct location, the printer will do a poor job of producing halftones.

While laser printers can produce colors other than black (provided you have a cartridge with colored toner), multiple-color printing is difficult using xerography. Nevertheless, color laser printers are available, though at substantially higher prices than black-and-white printers. For controlling color printing, the PostScript description language includes operators for specifying shade, hue, and brightness on a pixel-by-pixel basis.

Imaging Mechanisms

Engineers refer to the laser as a "flying spot" imaging mechanism, because a single source of light moves back and forth rapidly across the drum. The laser itself does not move; rather, a spinning mirror directs the beam across the drum.

As an alternative to lasers many manufacturers are using other light sources, including light emitting diodes (LED's), liquid crystal shutters (LCS's), and cathode ray tubes (CRT's). All these methods are described as *electrophotographic* because they produce a charge on the drum using some type of light source. A typical LED array incorporates about 2400 miniature LED's set in a row the width of the paper; each is independently controlled by the printer's internal computer. As the printer drum rotates, the LED's turn on and off up to 26,000 times per minute. A lens focuses the light onto the drum, which acquires a charge where the light strikes.

The LCS mechanism works in a similar manner. Thousands of individual liquid crystal shutters are set in an array. A light source is positioned behind the LCS array. When current is applied to the LCS, it becomes transparent; when current is removed, it becomes opaque. In this way the light beam is either allowed through to the printer drum or else blocked.

The advantage of LED or LCS array printers over printers that use lasers is that they have fewer moving parts. The disadvantage is that a single failed LED or LCS will cause streaking, which is particularly noticeable in graphics printing. The chance that any given LED or LCS will fail in a year's time is quite small, but the probability of at least one failure an entire array of 2400 is much higher. If a malfunction does occur, most array printers are designed so that you can replace the entire array by removing several screws.

CRT printers are based on a single-line CRT. An electron beam flashes across the length of the CRT, turning on pin points of blue light, which activate dots on the print drum. An advantage of the CRT technology is that the coating material used on print drums is most receptive to the blue light that only CRT's offer, which means that less light is needed to activate dots on the drum and the drum's life is prolonged. Price has prevented the CRT from becoming a popular option. Quality is also a matter of question, since magnetic fields generated by the printer can distort the electronic beam inside the CRT.

Other processes have been developed which use methods other than light focused on a photosensitive drum. One such nonxerographic technology is *magnetographic* printing, in which a charge is written onto the print drum using methods similar to those used by the writing heads on disk drives. The magnetically charged dots pick up toner that has a slight iron content. One advantage of the method is that the image on the drum is more stable than with electrophotographic drums. A pattern can be built up on the drum in several passes, which means that the printer controller can build the image in sections and hence can get by with less memory.

Ion-deposition printers bombard the print drum with charged particles rather than light. The advantage is that the ion drum can be a steel surface, more durable than the light-sensitive drums or belts used by xerographic machines. Ion-deposition printers tend to be priced too high to be considered desktop publishing tools. Their forte is high-speed output; quality tends to be somewhat lower than that of laser printers.

Thermal-magnetic-optical (TMO) printers work in a fashion similar to LCS array printers. A magnetic material, when heated, can be made rapidly either to block or transmit polarized light, according to an electronic signal. One TMO method, *electro-erosion*, requires the use of aluminized paper. As the paper passes under a set of tiny electrodes, the printer vaporizes the shiny coating to create dots of black. This method has been used for 600-dpi printers, suitable for typesetting.

Although other exotic printing technologies will no doubt appear, improvements are most likely to come not as a result of entirely new imaging technologies, but rather from refinements of existing methods that will allow cheaper production of laser printers. The importance of manufacturing economies rather than absolute technological superiority is indicated by the fact that printer manufacturers have tended to choose imaging methods based on technologies in which they already have a manufacturing advantage. Canon, for example, with strength in producing mirrors and lenses due to its camera manufacturing, chose a laser as the imaging mechanism in its printers. Casio, as the world's largest producer of liquid crystals for watches, calculators, and computer displays, chose to use LCS arrays.

Not to be excluded from the list of options are two technologies normally associated with lower-resolution printers—*ink jet* and *dot matrix*. Under continual refinement, both are beginning to encroach on the 300-dpi mark formerly the exclusive province of laser printers. Dot matrix printers capable of 240 dpi have been on the market for several years. These printers tend to be less expensive than electrophotographic printers; the trade-off, of course, is speed. Ink jet printers, on the other hand, have demonstrated speeds and resolutions comparable to those of laser printers. Moreover, ink jet printers can more easily produce color output. Due to the rapidly dropping prices for laser printers, however, it is unlikely that either dot matrix or ink jet printers will play more than a minor role in desktop publishing systems.

Raster Image Processor

The typical laser printer prints one page in as little as eight seconds. In that time, a bit map of the entire page—approximately nine million on and off signals—must be sent to the imaging mechanism. Orchestrating this complex task is the job of the raster image processor (RIP), also known as the *printer controller.*

Despite the large number of models of laser printers available, only a small number of companies manufacture the printing engine itself. For example, over 40 companies use the Canon LBP-CX engine in their laser printers, including Apple, Hewlett-Packard, and Cordata. Thus, the differences in capabilities between the printers made by these companies is entirely the result of differences in the RIP, which each company designs for its own product.

The RIP is, quite literally, a computer. It has all the elements of a standard microcomputer: a central processing unit (the brains); permanent memory or ROM (read-only memory); dynamic memory or RAM (random access memory); and interfaces for data exchange (see Figure 8-1). The only way that the computer differs from a normal personal computer is that it lacks its own disk drives, keyboard, and display, and it is dedicated to the single purpose of controlling printing.

Every RIP has a set of internal software programs for handling the printing task, known as a page description language. Because the capabilities of this internal software are the principal factor determining what can be accomplished on a given printer, Chapter 10 is devoted to this topic.

Central processing unit:
- sorts incoming stream of data into text, bit-mapped graphics, page description language commands
- executes printer protocols or commands of page description language
- generates stream of signals to send to imaging mechanism

Dynamic memory (RAM):
- stores bit map of the page
- maintains a cache of character bit maps computed from outlines
- stores downloaded graphic images
- stores downloaded fonts in bit-map or outline form
- performs miscellaneous temporary storage functions for the central processing unit
- stores sets of commands under macro headings

Permanent memory (ROM):
- stores printer operating system and page description language
- stores fonts in outline or bit-map form

Figure 8-1 *Functions of parts of the raster image processor.*

The RIP need not be physically located within the printer. Some printers have an on-board microprocessor and some RAM and ROM, but borrow additional RAM from the computer driving the printer. In other designs the entire RIP is located on a circuit board installed in the computer. The main advantage of the latter approach is that it allows the printer to share resources such as RAM with the computer; the disadvantage is that it may tie up these resources, locking up the computer while pages are being constructed.

Permanent and Dynamic Memory

Both permanent and dynamic memory (ROM and RAM) serve multiple purposes in the operation of a laser printer. The foremost function of ROM is to store the page description language used by the RIP to run the laser printer. Another use for

ROM is to store fonts. Some laser printer designs allow the variety of fonts available to the printer to be expanded via plug-in ROM cartridges. As described in Chapter 9, fonts may be stored in either bit-map or outline form.

In the case of a bit-map font, the pattern of dots that produces a given character is stored in memory as an identical pattern of digital bits. For outline fonts, each character is stored in memory in the form of a mathematical description of the lines and curves that join to form its shape. The mathematical description of a character must be processed and converted to a bit map prior to printing, a process handled by the RIP. Although not all page description languages are capable of handling fonts stored in outline form, the method is powerful because it enables characters of any size to be generated from a single set of outlines for that typeface.

The amount of RAM varies from only 50 kilobytes in some printers to eight megabytes or more. Since it is easily written to and just as easily erased, RAM serves a variety of functions. Some RIP's build a full-page bit map in RAM, which is then transmitted to the imaging mechanism. This method speeds up operation, since the RIP can be building the bit map of a new page in one section of memory while the bit map of the previous page is being transmitted to the imaging mechanism, but it requires that the printer have at least one megabyte of RAM (the amount necessary to store an entire page at full 300-dpi resolution).

RAM may also be used for storing fonts in various forms. For example, some printers allow fonts to be downloaded into the printer from storage on a floppy or hard disk. For printers that store fonts as outlines in ROM, RAM may be used to provide a cache for font bit maps. The first time the printer prints a character, it generates the bit map and stores a copy of it in the cache. Thereafter, whenever that character needs to be printed, the printer can retrieve the bit map from the cache. Using a cache increases the speed at which text can be printed, since generating the bit map of a character from an outline is a fairly time-consuming process.

Besides storing bit maps of fonts, RAM can store graphic images or complex sets of commands under a single name as a *macro* or a *procedure* (depending on the terminology used by your printer). Thereafter, the image can be printed or the set of commands can be executed by issuing the name of the macro or procedure.

Printers with less than a megabyte of RAM cannot print a full page of graphics unless they print them at lower than 300-dpi resolution. Having more than a megabyte allows such added capabilities as loading multiple fonts and macros into the printer. Fortunately, prices of RAM have tumbled in recent years to the point where a megabyte or more is no longer prohibitively expensive.

The Printer/Computer Interface

The interface between the printer and the computer is a two-way highway through which the computer conveys text, graphics, and images in various forms and through which the printer confirms that data has been received.

Such interfaces are of two general types: *parallel* and *serial*. In a serial interface, such as the RS-232C standard, data is transferred along a single path, one bit at a time. Parallel paths, as the name implies, provide multiple channels for seven or eight bits to be transferred simultaneously. Depending on the computer and the laser printer, parallel transmission ranges from two to eight times as fast as serial.

As it receives a stream of data from the front-end computer, the printer first must sort it into three types of information: text, raster graphics, and commands. When the computer is transferring text, data is sent one byte at a time, each byte representing a single number between 0 and 127 or between 0 and 255, depending on whether the printer recognizes seven-bit or eight-bit bytes.

In theory, any character can be assigned to any number, but most printers follow the ASCII coding scheme for numbers between 0 and 127. The ASCII standard assigns commonly used functions such as line feed or carriage return to the numbers from 0 to 32. The numbers from 33 to 127 are used for the letters, numbers, and punctuation marks found on a typical keyboard.

Between 128 and 255, called *high-bit ASCII* or simply *high-bit* characters (so called because to represent such characters the eighth bit of each byte is always turned on), the coding scheme is not standardized. Depending on the font being used by the printer, the high bits may be used for storing foreign characters, graphics characters, or special math or other symbols. The particular set of symbols that are assigned to numbers between 0 and 127 or 0 and 255 are referred to as the *symbol set*. Common symbol sets are the PC symbol set used by IBM and the Roman-8 symbol set used by Hewlett-Packard.

Raster graphics is the simplest type of information transmitted from computer to printer, since very little processing is required of the raster image processor before passing the data on to the imaging mechanism. For raster graphics, 1's and 0's in the data stream are converted into on or off signals to the imaging mechanism, producing a pattern of black and white on the page. The computer must precede the stream of raster graphics data with a command indicating raster mode and specifying the location of the raster image on the page.

The third type of data is commands understood by the printer's page description language. Such commands are preceded by a special control character indicating that the data to follow is to be treated as commands rather than text or raster graphics. Once interpreted by the raster image processor, such commands may apply to formatting text, building graphic shapes from the graphics primitives provided by the page description language, management of fonts, paper feeds, and other printer functions.

A typical data-transfer rate for a printer using a serial connection is 9600 bits per second (bps). At this rate, 1200 bytes, or characters, are sent from the computer to the printer each second, approximately the number of characters on a double-spaced page of typewritten text. When the actual text to be printed is interspersed with formatting commands, transmission of a page of actual text may require up to several seconds, but even a relatively complex text page can be transmitted fairly quickly.

Not so with drawings or digitized images. At 300 dpi (90,000 dots per square inch), an 8-inch by 10-inch image comprises about seven million dots, each of which must be individually transferred as a data bit. At 9200 bps, such an image takes 13 minutes to send to the printer. Suppose you had a single page, half of which was taken up by text, the other half by a digitized picture. The entire page would take about six and a half minutes to transmit, out of which only about a second would be used for transmitting the text portion.

There are several ways of overcoming the time-consuming demands of graphics transmission. One is the use of a *printer buffer,* a segment of memory devoted to holding data for the printer. This does not speed up transmission, but at least it frees the computer for other uses while the image is being sent. Another innovation is the use of an ultra-high-speed interface between the portion of the computer's memory in which the graphic image is stored and the imaging mechanism of the printer. For sending a large volume of data, such an interface may simply bypass the RIP and take over control of the imaging mechanism. A manually operated switch returns control to the RIP. Yet another method is to use a data compression program to reduce the amount of data necessary to transmit an image. The amount of compression will vary considerably depending on the complexity of the image.

Choosing a Printer

In judging among printers, there are two sets of factors to consider. One set relates to the capabilities of the printer for handling text, graphics, and digitized images. Since these factors depend on the page description language or printer protocol used by the printer, they are discussed separately in Chapter 10. Other factors are listed below.

Speed   Printer vendors typically advertise the rated speed of the engine used in the printer. The problem with this figure is that it has little relation to the actual performance of the printer. Some printers do perform at close to the rated speed of the engine; others only perform at close to that speed when printing multiple copies of the same page; yet others are much slower than the rated speed no matter what they are printing. If speed is of importance to you, prepare a set of three benchmark tests to try before you buy: (1) ten copies of a one-page text document, (2) one copy of a ten-page text document, and (3) a graphic image.

Paper Handling   To meet the needs of organizations with several sizes and types of paper, some laser printers are equipped with multiple paper bins. Other paper-handling niceties include large input and output trays, the ability to output pages of a document in correct order, and collating.

Operating Cost   Some laser printers, such as the popular Canon LBP-CX used in the Apple LaserWriter, Hewlett-Packard LaserJet, and other models, use a single electrophotographic cartridge (called the EP cartridge) that is replaced every 3000 to 5000 copies, depending on the amount of toner used on each page. The EP cartridge includes the printer drum, developer, and toner. Other laser printer designs separate the toner cartridge from the drum and developer cartridge, and allow the latter to be replaced much less frequently. As a result, such designs may (depending on the price of toner) offer less expensive printing per page.

Print Quality   Two printers that operate at identical resolution may have quite different print qualities due to differences in the shapes of the dots. When comparing printers, inspect both text and graphic samples. Also, if you will be printing graphics, ask to see a page printed in solid black; some printers are poor at laying down even, dark black.

Interface Speed   The speed of the interface between the printer and the computer is not crucial for text applications, but is very much so for graphics. If you plan to print graphics, try to find a printer that has as an option a faster interface than the standard 9600-bps serial rate used by most laser printers, preferably one allowing parallel transmission.

Scanners

Scanners, also called digitizers, come in a variety of shapes and sizes. Flatbed scanners look like copiers—you lay the image to be scanned on a pane of glass and place a light-shielding flap over the top. Other scanners use a sheet-feed mechanism. A third variety is in the form of a stand-alone box that processes the signal produced by a video camera. One ingeniously-designed scanner from Thunder-Ware, called ThunderScan, snaps onto the Apple ImageWriter dot matrix printer, replacing the ribbon cartridge.

Whatever its outward appearance, any scanner uses either of two technologies for sampling an image: optical or video. Video scanners, which in general are less expensive and operate at lower resolution, use a standard video camera to record the image. Besides their lower resolution, video systems require more work to set up and careful attention to lighting. On the other hand, unlike optical scanners, they can be used to digitize a three-dimensional image. Optical scanners offer easier operation and higher resolution. On the other hand, optical scanners are limited to recording two-dimensional images, and they tend to be more expensive. Typical prices for video scanners (not including the video camera) are in the $350 range. Most flatbed optical scanners designed for use with microcomputers are in the $1500 to $3000 range.

The smallest area that the digitizer treats as a distinct unit is called a *pixel* (or *pel*), which stands for *picture element*. Typical sampling resolution for video scanners is 75 pixels per inch, although that figure can be upped by replacing the standard camera lens with a higher quality lens. Optical scanners typically sample at 300 pixels per inch.

Whatever their form, scanners perform a common function: reducing the continuous tones of an to an array of discrete numbers, each representing the shade of gray measured by the digitizer for a particular pixel. The number of levels of gray that are used to produce an image (the grayscale) varies, depending on the scanners; some offer only 8 levels, others as many as 256. Having been converted into such a grid, the image can be processed within the scanner, the computer, or the laser printer. Thus, a prime consideration in purchasing a scanner is whether it is compatible with your graphics software.

Since the amount of grayscale data contained in a single picture is quite large, scanners need to be used in conjunction with a mass storage device. Processing of scanned images is discussed in detail in Chapter 11.

Scanners have two additional applications. The first is converting line art into digital form. Digitizing a piece of line art allows it to be scaled, cropped, edited with a drawing program, and merged into text with a page makeup program. The second application is optical character recognition (OCR), "reading" typed or printed pages and converting them into the standard ASCII format usable by word processing and other programs. To be able to read text, the scanner must be equipped with character recognition software. Such software is generally capable of handling a limited set of typefaces, although systems allow you to "train" the scanner to recognize additional ones.

Because of the wide variation in scanner features and prices, you need to take care in selecting a model that meets your needs. One obvious consideration is scanning speed, which may vary from 12 seconds to half an hour per page. Another is degree of control over parameters such as halftone patterns, contrast, and brightness.

Two features can greatly add to the convenience of a scanning system. The first is the ability to view and crop an image on screen before it is digitized. This not only lowers the time needed to scan an image, but also reduces the amount of storage needed to save the file. The second time-saving feature is the capability to adjust such parameters as contrast after scanning, rather than having to redigitize an image every time you want to make an adjustment.

Personal Computers

Any sort of computer—from the most inexpensive microcomputer to the largest mainframe—can be used as the hub of a publishing system. That's not to say that any sort of computer is up to the demands of a particular type of publishing project. Whether a given computer is appropriate for a given publishing application depends on three major factors: the type of user interface provided by the computer; the computational power, memory, and storage; and the availability of software that is appropriate to the nature of the job.

The Macintosh

Several aspects of the design of the Macintosh make it ideal for desktop publishing applications, particularly for page makeup programs that allow on-screen layout of text and graphics. Other personal computers, such as the IBM PC, require expensive retrofitting to match what comes as standard equipment on the Macintosh. Built into the computer's crisp, bit-mapped display is an underlying set of powerful graphics commands known as QuickDraw. With these routines, software developers can write programs that include powerful text and graphics manipulations. Moreover, this standard graphics environment assures a level of compatibility among all all Macintosh programs.

Through its ability to open multiple windows on-screen, clipping a graphic or a segment of text from one program and inserting it into another is fairly easy on the Macintosh. The mouse allows easy positioning of graphics and text. And finally, the "desktop metaphor" interface, with its icons and pull-down menus, provides all applications with a similar command structure, making the computer easy to use. All of these elements together make the Macintosh well suited both for text-oriented publishing and page makeup applications that integrate text and graphics.

Despite its good fit for desktop publishing, the Macintosh has several drawbacks. The first is the lack of compatibility between its operating system and the predominant MS-DOS operating system. In most organizations, the bulk of word processing is done on DOS computers. Moving documents from DOS formats into the Macintosh for page makeup is an inconvenience at best. A second problem is the lack of *multitasking*, that is, the ability to run more than one application at a time. Multitasking greatly eases the work involved in merging results from one program with those of another. For example, with your graphics program running in one window and your page makeup program in another, you can alter the size of an ill-fitting graph or drawing without leaving the page makeup program.

MS-DOS Computers

In most organizations, the workhorse computers are members of the IBM PC family (including the PC, the PC XT, and the PC AT) or work-alikes using the same MS-DOS operating system. The suitability of these computers for desktop publishing depends on the nature of the publishing task at hand.

These computers can handle text-only tasks, such as word processing or typesetting, as well as simple graphics, such as rules and boxes that can be generated via commands within the text-handling application. But for applications that involve combining text with graphics created in separate applications, DOS systems present several obstacles.

First, unlike the Macintosh's Finder operating system, DOS does not allow you to easily enter, exit, and clip material between applications by opening and closing windows. While programs do exist for clipping a picture from one application, saving it in a file, and later inserting it in another document, the process is laborious and awkward.

Rather than supporting a single graphics standard, the PC now hosts a variety of graphics display options, creating numerous problems for software developers. For example, any software developer writing an application for the PC must create separate versions of the program for the standard IBM monochrome display (excellent for text, but with only rudimentary graphics display capabilities), the IBM Color Graphics Adapter, the Hercules black-and-white adapter, and the IBM Enhanced Graphics Adapter. Each display standard has a different resolution and set of color/black-and-white options. None provides the built-in graphics primitives that assist Macintosh software developers to deliver high performance.

The saving grace of IBM's approach to personal computers has been its devotion to upward compatibility, which allows more advanced computers to continue using older, but still popular programs, and the open-systems approach, which allows the basic configuration to be enhanced by the user. Consequently, the road is now open for upgrading DOS computers to systems quite suitable for Macintosh-style text/graphics publishing.

The key upgrade is Microsoft Windows, Digital Research's GEM, or a similar operating environment. Such a program allows the PC to perform the functions popularized by the Macintosh: cutting and pasting of text and graphics, viewing pages in more-or-less WYSIWYG form, and so on. Some, including Windows, offer multitasking, a capability absent on the Macintosh. If you're thinking of an upgrade, however, don't be deceived by the low price tag of the new interface. To get good performance from the windowing environment requires a substantially more powerful hardware configuration than that which is standard on the PC: additional RAM, particularly for multitasking; a hard disk; and a mouse. A graphics display is also necessary, as discussed in Chapter 11. To get adequate speed with

Microsoft Windows, you also need a faster central processing unit than the Intel 8088 chip found in the basic PC, such as the 80286 or the 80386. GEM, however, shows satisfactory performance with the PC.

Workstations

Workstations, also called *supermicros*, use microprocessor technology to achieve levels of performance previously associated with minicomputers and feature graphics interfaces similar to that of the Macintosh. These computers, made by Sun Microsystems, Apollo Computer, IBM, and others, provide full-page, high-resolution displays, fast processing, networking capabilities, and a multitasking operating system. Increasingly, the line between these expensive workstations and high-end personal computers is becoming blurred; workstation prices are dropping while personal computer performance increases. Like the Macintosh, supermicros use an operating system (usually UNIX) that may present compatibility problems with documents created on DOS computers. In many cases, however, add-on boards and software are available for translating files created by DOS applications such as MicroPro's WordStar for use by the workstation's own word processing and page makeup programs.

Chapter 9

How Computers Handle Fonts

Fonts for computerized typesetting systems consist of electronically stored data—data that describes in various ways the shapes of the characters that make up a typeface. Eventually, the typefaces are rendered as a *raster image*—a picture built from dots or as a series of scan lines, like a TV image.

The crudest example of a raster font is the familiar dot matrix printer fonts used by most inexpensive desktop printers. The resolution of these printers (typically 60 dpi) severely limits the possible designs of the letters. For a typical dot matrix printer, the letters are constructed on a 6-dot by 8-dot grid. This grid is reflected in the print head, which consists of a cluster of printing elements, usually in the form of small hammers, one for each dot on the grid. To print a letter, an array of hammers strikes the printer ribbon and the pattern describing that letter is imprinted on the paper. This grid, then, acts as a template, and every letter is described as a pattern of dots on that template. This is a simple illustration of a bit map. Each character is described by an array of bits—a series of on/off signals, each describing a dot or white spot in the grid, transmitted to the print head.

Laser printers are also digital printers, but with several very important differences from the impact dot matrix printers. First, the dots that build the grid array are much smaller and closer together, typically with 300 dots per inch. Second, the templates can be built to describe characters of variable size. Because it has no fixed-size print head, the laser printer is free to draw letters of any size. This freedom to draw characters of any size has some very important implications for the fonts laser printers use.

All digital typefaces can be described as arrays of dots. Figure 9-1 shows a character as it would be rasterized on a number of grids of varying resolution. The

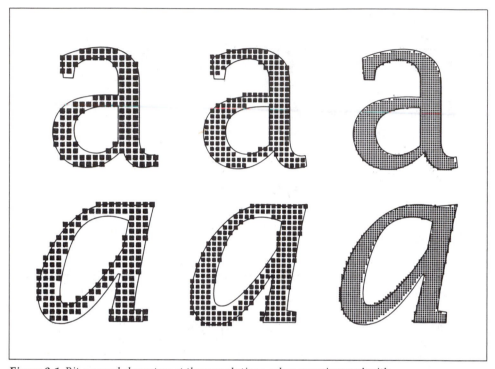

Figure 9-1 Bit-mapped characters at three resolutions, when superimposed with the outlines upon which they are based, illustrate how higher resolutions offer greater fidelity to original type designs. The more curves a character contains— as in the italic characters above—the more difficult it is to create a satisfactory rendering at low resolutions. (Courtesy Bigelow & Holmes)

more dots available in the grid (the higher the resolution), the smoother the contour of the letter becomes. Likewise, the more dots available, the more flexibility there is in the design of the font. If a font's character widths are based, for instance, on 100 units to the em, simple arithmetic dictates that setting an accurately rendered 6-point character necessitates a marking engine with 1200-dpi resolution. (In six-point type, one em equals 6 points, or about 1/12 inch. At this size, then, one typesetter unit is 1/1200 inch. For a concordance of one image dot per relative unit, a 1200-dpi marking resolution is necessary.) At any resolution below 1200 dpi, the marking engine must make some averaging corrections at the expense of image accuracy.

This problem has led to the development of typefaces designed specifically for use at laser printer resolutions. Notable among these is Lucida®, developed by

Charles Bigelow and Kris Holmes, whose character designs and stroke weights are optimized for legibility at 300-dpi resolution. Bigelow and Holmes have used the same traditional typographic and design concepts to develop a companion face—Pelucida®—for use on computer screens.

Bit-Mapped and Outline Fonts

The typesetting machine creates its character images based on information from the composed file prepared by the front-end computer. The fastest and easiest way for the typesetting machine to build characters is to have all of the fonts stored in bit-mapped form. Then all it has to do is pull the preformed bit maps from memory and image them as called for. Storing fonts as bit maps also allows the font designers to tackle problems like the 6-point letter mentioned above. Problem letters can be custom-built to allow for limited imaging abilities of the marking engine. The problem with this approach is storage.

Enormous areas of computer memory have to be reserved for font storage. At the relatively low resolution of 300 dpi (90,000 dots per square inch), this can vary from an inconvenience to a headache to a budget buster depending on how many typefaces and how many sizes a font library contains. At commercial resolutions of 1200 dpi (1.4 million dots per square inch) it becomes a veritable nightmare.

Digital typographers had to come up with some solution that was less memory-intensive than bit mapping every character in every desired point size. The answer was to describe the characters as outlines and then, like in a child's coloring book, fill them in with solid black. The beauty of the outline solution is that it allows the font designer to create one outline that can be mathematically enlarged or reduced. One outline can then be used to generate a wide range of type sizes.

The first scalable outline fonts were composed of straight-line segments, with curves described by a series of short straight line tangents in conjunction. In small type sizes, these straight-line segments blended together to give the eye the impression of smooth curves. In larger sizes, though, the component straight-line segments became visible, giving the characters a rough-hewn appearance.

As the technology of digital typography became more sophisticated, these tangent-based outlines yielded to outlines built with combinations of straight lines and mathematically expressed curves that smoothed out the characters' shapes. This straight-line/curve construction is an elegant solution to a thorny problem, but constructing fonts in this manner is very complex and time-consuming.

Most laser printer font manufacturers have opted for bit-mapped fonts because they are generally cheaper and easier to create, as are the software and printer controllers necessary to use them. In addition, laser printers were introduced to the market not as typesetting machines, but as improved office printers, and typographic flexibility was not part of the original plan.

Outline fonts, on the other hand, tend to be more expensive by virtue of the labor-intensity of their design and execution. Programs and typesetting machines that take advantage of scalable outline fonts, in turn, tend to be more complex and expensive as well. Furthermore, because scalable fonts provide much more flexibility, manufacturers feel justified in charging more for them.

Font Handling Systems

Although taken individually, bit-mapped fonts are generally less expensive than outline fonts, the economic issue is a cloudy one. If you plan to do a lot of varied typographic work, you may need a dozen or more sizes of a given typeface. If you are using bit-mapped fonts, this means that you will have to buy a dozen or more fonts. With outline fonts, you need to buy only one and scale it to the sizes you need. When all is said and done, the more expensive outline fonts may prove to be the more economical.

An important issue to consider when choosing a desktop publishing system is how much liberty it gives you to mix a number of fonts in the same document. This is contingent on how the fonts are stored. In commercial typesetting machines, fonts are typically stored on internal hard disks or on floppy disks that are mounted in the machine as a job demands. Laser printers, though, have a number of different font-handling strategies. Some laser printers use fonts stored on computer chips mounted in ROM (read-only memory) cartridges. The cartridges are loaded into the printer, and only the fonts present in the installed cartridge can be used.

The best systems allow you to download the fonts you need into the printer's memory. These systems allow you to mix and match as many and whatever fonts you want in a particular document, up to the limits imposed by available memory. Depending on the configuration of your system, you might download to the printer itself or to a segment of the host computer's memory allocated for that purpose.

As desktop publishing technology develops, laser printers will increasingly emulate the font-handling approaches of commercial typesetting systems in the use of hard and floppy drives for font storage. Page description languages, such as PostScript, DDL, and InterPress, are now creating a common ground that will allow desktop publishing systems to use fonts compatible with commercial typesetting machines. Considering how much money you can wind up investing in fonts, make sure that the ones you buy can grow along with you.

Another new force that is changing how typesetting machines use fonts are font manufacturing companies, including Xiphias, Bitstream, and Conographic Corporation. These vendors buck the trend among font manufacturers by disassociating themselves from hardware sales, preferring to sell digital fonts in a number of formats that hardware manufacturers can adapt to their own uses. By acting as central font developers, they allow system manufacturers to avoid having to reinvent existing font libraries. Having a shared font developer also raises the promise that many systems may use the exact same fonts, allowing the free passage of formatted documents from one system to another.

Font Editing Software

A useful addition to your font library may be a font editing program. These programs are available for use with both scalable and bit-mapped fonts. They enable you to change the shapes of existing characters by either editing the bit-mapped images themselves or by altering the outlines from which the character images are generated. Few manufacturers' fonts can be altered with such software, though, because if you can alter the designs you could presumably steal them as well.

The most popular role of these programs is likely to be in the creation of characters that can be associated with a font that already exists. A typical application would be creating your company logo using the font editor, and linking the logo to your standard fonts so that it could be accessed with one keystroke, just like a letter of the alphabet.

Naturally, font editors can also be used to create entirely new fonts, and you can use them to design your own typefaces. It is doubtful that you would ever do this, but an attempt at it will no doubt increase your appreciation for the skill and artistry demanded by this difficult craft.

Chapter 10

Foundation Software

Laser printers differ from other printers used in offices in one major respect: built into the printer is a microcomputer that runs a set of internal programs. This internal software functions as a foundation for applications such as word processing or page makeup programs. Receiving instructions from an application, the page description language generates the stream of bits that control the printer's imaging mechanism.

Even though it is transparent to the user of a desktop publishing system, the page description language is the system's most critical component. Understanding the differences between such languages is vital in choosing printers and determining what a given software application might be expected to accomplish.

Languages vary widely in their ability to handle text, graphics, and halftone images. Some can print characters at all sizes and orientations, others at only a limited number of fixed sizes and in only one or two orientations. Some include numerous built-in commands for creating complex graphic shapes; others are capable of only simple line segments and rectangles.

The design of the page description language also affects the speed of the printer, the variety of typefaces available to it, and the number of programs that can be used with it. Finally, some page description languages provide device and resolution independence. This means you can create a draft copy of your manuscript on a laser printer made by one manufacturer and then print out a camera-ready version on a phototypesetting machine made by a different company, as long as both machines incorporate the same language.

Static and Dynamic Languages

Currently, page description languages come in two types: *static* and *dynamic*. The vocabulary of a static language cannot be extended by defining new words from the old ones, as is possible with dynamic languages. In the hierarchy of computer-programming languages, static page description languages are a sort of baby talk—sets of words with only a rudimentary grammar.

The printer protocols used by dot matrix and daisy-wheel printers, such as the Diablo and Epson protocols, are the simplest examples of static languages. Some vendors offer laser printers that use these protocols (often as an optional mode alongside a more powerful page description language). The advantage of an established protocol such as the Diablo or Epson standard is that a laser printer that uses it is compatible with any of the thousands of programs that have been written for that protocol. The disadvantage is that the protocols designed for daisy-wheel and dot matrix printers do not address the more advanced capabilities of laser printers. They represent a least-common-denominator approach, limited to printing monospaced text or simple graphics and not allowing for multiple fonts. Thus, laser printers that go no further than merely emulating dot matrix and letter-quality printers are not really desktop publishing tools.

A slightly more ambitious approach is for a manufacturer to adopt an existing printer protocol and then add new operations specifically for laser printers. The resulting page description language is still static, but at least it includes some operations to tap the greater powers of laser printing. An example of this approach is Hewlett-Packard's Printer Command Language (PCL).

Because PCL provides a superset of protocols used by H-P's earlier dot matrix and daisy-wheel printers, any software written for those machines can be used by an H-P laser printer without modification. Conversely, a program written for an H-P laser printer can also be used with less sophisticated printers; those operations not executable by the lower-level printer are simply ignored.

Like static languages, dynamic languages provide commands for invoking common printer functions; they differ from static languages in that they are extensible, that is, commands can be combined in a flexible manner to form new commands. The most well-known dynamic languages are PostScript, DDL, and Inter-Press. While static languages are limited to the specific operations built into the language by its designers, the operations that can be performed by a dynamic language are virtually unlimited.

A Feature Checklist

The distinction between static and dynamic page description languages is an important one to make, but it does not completely characterize the powers of a language. For example, a sufficiently full-featured static language may provide functionality for certain applications that is as good as or better than a dynamic language. To distinguish among languages, it is necessary to look at some specifics: their device independence, the quality of the fonts they use, their character-manipulating capabilities, their graphics primitives, their image-processing capabilities, their document-handling features, and their programmability.

Device Independence   Page description languages that run on a variety of different printers and typesetting machines are called device independent. In working with an application that uses a device-independent language, you need not concern yourself with the resolution of the printer, since the language optimizes the printed output according to the specific capabilities of the device.

The benefits of device independence are threefold. First, for software developers it eases the work of creating drivers, the instructions that translate the output of a program into a form usable by a particular printer. For example, with PostScript, the same driver can be used with either the 300-dpi Apple LaserWriter printer or the 2540-dpi Linotronic 300 typesetter. Second, it allows the laser printer to be used as a proofing machine in conjunction with a typesetting machine. Third, it gives you the freedom to mix and match equipment from various manufacturers in creating a desktop publishing system.

Quality and Variety of Fonts   Those page description languages that allow you to work with outline fonts have a definite edge, because they allow you to generate fonts of any size from a single outline. With bit-mapped fonts, you are likely to find that even a fairly large collection will lack sizes you need from time to time, especially when it comes to large display faces. Variety of typefaces is also a consideration. The more widely accepted the page description language, the more likely it is that third-party font companies have created large libraries of typefaces for it. For example, at this writing at least four companies besides Hewlett-Packard were creating typefaces in a format usable by H-P's PCL. On the other hand, quantity is not the same as quality. Look for fonts licensed from established font foundries, such as the ITC and Mergenthaler libraries.

Character-Manipulating Capabilities   Languages designed for use with bit-mapped fonts tend to have much more limited character-manipulating capabilities than those designed for outline fonts. With some languages using bit-mapped fonts, you are limited to printing characters in upright orientation; with others, you can print at 90-, 180-, and 270-degree rotations.

With outline fonts, the possibilities for character manipulation are virtually endless. Characters can be scaled, stretched, rotated to any orientation, filled with any shade or pattern, and obliqued. Figure 10-1 shows some character manipulations produced with PostScript.

Graphics   The ability of a laser printer to print graphics depends on the power and versatility of the graphics commands provided by the page description language. The best printers offer page description languages that provide numerous operators, or commands, for manipulating graphics. Dynamic languages are particularly suited for graphics, because they also allow you to define entirely new

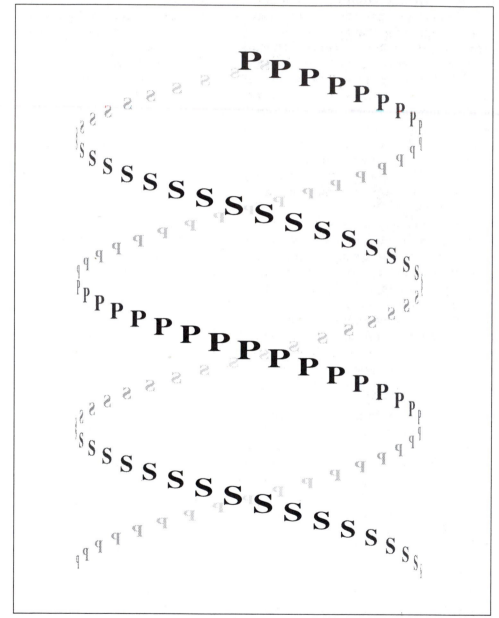

Figure 10-1 *Using a single master typeface outline, PostScript can generate type of various sizes and fill it with shades or patterns.*

graphics operations for particular purposes. Printers with less flexible languages support only simple bars, lines, and shading, or no graphics at all. The following is an inventory of types of operations needed for printing graphics.

• *Lines and Rules:* All page description languages provide some commands for printing line segments or rules. Some also let you specify the thickness and the pattern or shade of gray of the rule.

• *Patterns:* Some languages provide a limited set of predefined patterns for use in shading; others allow you to create additional custom patterns.

• *Shading:* Some languages provide a fixed number of gray shades, others as many shades as can be rendered by the printer.

• *Corners and Line Ends:* For joining line segments at other than right angles, some languages provide special corner commands that let you specify rounded, jointed, or squared-off corners.

• *Arcs and Curves:* With more advanced languages, simple as well as complex types of arcs and curves can be specified. These commands allow printing of ovals and circles.

• *Working with Arbitrary Regions:* A powerful graphics feature is the ability to define an arbitrary region on the page—such as the outline of a large character—and then apply graphics commands to it, such as stretching, rotating, copying, moving, and filling with a pattern or shade.

Image Processing   As described in Chapter 11, laser printers render photographs and other images as patterns of dots, with shades of gray simulated either by patterns of varying densities or by clumps of dots of varying sizes. To print such an image, most page description languages must receive a full bit map of the image; in other words, for every dot to be printed on paper, the printer must receive an electronic signal. A few languages provide a more sophisticated type of image processing. Rather than receive a complete bit map of the image to be printed, printers equipped with such languages are sent the grid of grayscale values produced by the scanner. The language then generates a final bit map in a manner that is optimized for the resolution and dot characteristics of a particular device. Typically, the manufacturer of the laser printer will determine default parameters for the imaging commands; these can then be altered by the user of the system to create special graphic effects.

Document Handling   Although, as the name suggests, the emphasis of page description languages is on the single page, some languages have special instructions for controlling multiple-document printing, a type of work that is mainly done by expensive, high-speed laser printers used with networked computers. InterPress and DDL both provide such controls as the ability to specify the order in which pages are printed, production of 2-up or 16-up signatures, and 2-sided printing.

Programmability   The most elementary sort of programmability offered by page description languages are macros. Macros allow you to specify a string of commands that is stored in the laser printer's memory and assigned a name. When you issue the name of the macro, the string of commands is executed. Most static languages offer some sort of macro capability, though they may limit you to using a small number of macros at a time.

Dynamic languages offer the types of programmability found in standard computer languages: conditional statements, looping, and the ability to combine commands into new ones. It is programmability, combined with sophisticated graphics operations, such as the ability to work with arbitrary regions, that most significantly distinguishes the high end from the low end of page description languages.

For example, with most static page description languages it would be possible for a graphics application to include a command such as BOX A B C D E, where A is the thickness of the rule surrounding the box, B and C are the coordinates of the upper-left corner, and D and E are the height and width, respectively. But only with a dynamic page description language would it be possible to define a flexible command such as NEXTBOX A, which measures the size of the next A paragraphs following the command and draws a box around them.

PostScript

Developed by Adobe Systems, PostScript is currently the leading page description language, the standard to which more recent arrivals must be compared. Adobe does not manufacture printers itself, but rather licenses PostScript to other vendors including, Linotype, Apple, Digital Equipment Corporation, QMS, and Texas Instruments. Among its considerable strengths are device independence (PostScript equipment ranges from the 300-dpi Apple LaserWriter to the 2540-dpi Linotronic 300 typesetting machine); outline fonts licensed from the extensive International Typeface Corporation and Mergenthaler, Stempel, Haas collections; extensibility; and powerful graphics and text-processing capabilities.

The principal concept underlying PostScript is that text, graphics, and digitized image handling should all be based on the same model. Thus, at the outset PostScript defies the traditional division between graphics-oriented and text-oriented printers and software. For example, characters are created as outlines, using graphics primitives such as line segments, arcs, curves, and several kinds of joints. Once an outline has been created from a combination of primitives, it can be filled in with a shade or pattern, clipped and moved or copied, scaled, stretched, or rotated, as in Figure 10-2.

Because typefaces are stored by PostScript as sets of character outlines, any graphics operation can be applied to text. From a practical standpoint, treating text

Figure 10-2 *PostScript's outline fonts can be rotated, as shown in this spiral.*

as graphics at all times would result in excessively slow printer operation. To increase text-handling speed, PostScript provides some special text operations. For example, it uses a character cache to increase printing speed. It only computes a character's bit map from its outline the first time it receives it. When the character is encountered a second time, PostScript retrieves the already-calculated bit map rather than recalculating it. Printing a character from a bit map stored in a cache is literally about a thousand times faster than calculating and printing it from the outline.

For rendering halftone images, PostScript can receive the data produced by a digitizer—strings of numbers representing the grayscale value of each pixel in an array. It can then convert this information into the digital equivalent of a photographic halftone screen, whose resolution and angle are adjusted to produce optimal results on a given type of marking engine, from low-resolution laser printers to high-resolution phototypesetters. It also lets you use various sorts of patterns to simulate shades of gray, including synthetic line screens or dot screens.

Besides operators for graphics, text, and images, PostScript provides operators for manipulating the coordinate system of the page. Using the language it is very easy, for example, to tilt an entire page of text at a 20-degree angle. More complex transformations of the coordinate system are also possible, such as wrapping it around an imaginary cylinder.

One of the main consequences of PostScript's way of handling text, graphics, and images is device independence. Since characters are handled as outlines, the application can ignore the question about whether they will be printed on a 300-dpi laser printer or a 2200-dpi phototypesetting machine. The same goes for graphics and halftones, since the graphics primitives and halftone screens that provide the basis for generating line art and halftones are both specified in a manner independent of output resolution.

Along with device independence comes independence from any particular vendor, since Adobe Systems licenses PostScript to a variety of equipment manufacturers. In the past, vendors of typesetting systems tended to lock their customers into their own machines and software because of the incompatibility of those systems with any others. PostScript, however, makes it possible to mix and match the best software and hardware for a particular set of needs, regardless of who makes the products—as long as they all use PostScript.

DDL

Created by Imagen, DDL has many of the same features found in PostScript and InterPress, including a wide range of graphics operations, extensibility, and the ability to scale fonts to different sizes. Font vendors from whom Imagen has licensed fonts include Linotype and Bigelow & Holmes. DDL also offers some unique features, such as the manner in which it scales fonts. In traditional typography, it was found that the appearance of typefaces improved if their height-to-width ratio was allowed to increase slightly in larger point sizes. DDL reproduces this effect by applying a slightly larger scaling factor to height than to width.

DDL also includes some key features designed to improve execution speed. These include caching of graphic bit maps as well as font bit maps, and several techniques for reducing the size of document files and speeding transmission from computer to printer.

Despite Imagen's intent to not only match but to improve upon the features of PostScript, at this writing DDL was not yet available in any products, though both Hewlett-Packard and Imagen had stated their intent to market DDL printers. Because DDL is starting the race about two years behind PostScript, it remains to be seen whether the language will attract software vendors to write DDL drivers for their applications and additional hardware vendors (especially those selling phototypesetting machines) to offer DDL equipment.

InterPress

Prior to founding Adobe Systems, the designers of PostScript were involved in the development of Xerox's InterPress, and the kinship between the two languages is evident: the most recent specification of the InterPress language, version 3.0, includes many of the advanced capabilities found in PostScript, including extensible commands, programmability, and powerful graphics operations. Implementation of the full specification has been slow, however, so its popularity has been constrained. At this writing, InterPress had not been implemented on equipment by any vendors other than Xerox itself.

Version 3.0 actually comprises three versions. The Professional Graphics Set, the most powerful of the three, is comparable to PostScript, providing such advanced features as arbitrary rotations and ability to apply graphics operations such as cutting and pasting to regions with arbitrary boundaries. The Publication Set is a subset of the Professional Graphics Set, lacking the ability to perform arbitrary rotations and definition of regions with arbitrary boundaries. Instead, rotations are limited to 90, 180, and 270 degrees, and graphics operations such as cutting and pasting can only be applied to rectangular regions. The Commercial Set, a subset of the Publication Set, lacks graphics commands except for simple rules, but does support printing of scanned graphics.

While the InterPress standard provides for the use of outline fonts, current implementations use only Xerox's own bit-mapped fonts. However, the company has defined a Font Interchange Standard for future font development, to which several companies have committed themselves, including Bitstream, Linotype, and Compugraphic.

A strong point in favor of InterPress is its document-handling capabilities, tailored for expensive, high-speed laser printers such as the Xerox 9700, which can print 120 pages per minute. While printers in the 8- to 24-page-per-minute range are normally used for creating single copies or master copies, high-speed printers such as the 9700 are used for multiple-copy document production. Hence, the InterPress language includes features such as the ability to print large signatures and to control collating.

H-P Printer Command Language

A static language with no extensibility or programmability, Hewlett-Packard's Printer Command Language is important because of the popularity of the LaserJet family of printers on which it was originally introduced. Because of the large number of software companies that have created PCL drivers, other laser printer vendors have found it convenient to offer PCL as an optional language on their own machines; hence PCL has become a de facto standard for low-end laser printers.

PCL allows pages to be printed in either upright or sideways orientation. Graphics commands include horizontal and vertical rules and rectangular shading with patterns or grays. The language does not support arcs or circles.

Fonts for PCL must be in bit-mapped form, and can either be on ROM cartridges or downloaded into the printer's memory. The language does not allow graphics manipulations such as scaling, obliquing, rotating, or shading to be applied to fonts. Since a separate set of bit maps must be stored for each point size and orientation of a given typeface, PCL's approach limits the variety of fonts available to an application. On the other hand, because of its wide adoption, font availability is good for PCL, with fonts offered by Hewlett-Packard and a number of third-party vendors.

PCL's support for printing digitized images is rudimentary. It cannot handle grayscale values for halftone pixels, but only black-or-white pixel data. Each pixel received is then printed as a clump of either one, four, nine, or sixteen spots, depending on the resolution specified. This allows drawings and halftones to be printed at different sizes, but only by varying the resolution.

Since PCL allows flexible control over the horizontal and vertical positioning of text, it is capable of supporting the formatting demands of typesetting programs. Macros can also be created, allowing groups of commands to be named and then saved in the printer's dynamic memory. This feature provides a convenient way of storing frequently used graphic images or page descriptions, such as those used to specify a form, which can then be combined with text. For example, a letterhead, including a corporate logo, might be stored in the printer as a macro and then printed automatically on every sheet of correspondence produced by the company.

Although the operations built into PCL are fairly circumscribed, they do provide sufficient functions for many text-only publishing applications and for documents that combine text with simple bar-chart business graphics. More ambitious types of pages can be printed, but only if the host application assumes the work of generating the appropriate bit map in the computer's memory and then spoon-feeding it bit by bit to the printer. Generating such bit maps is beyond the reach of most applications; moreover, transferring them to the printer tends to take an inordinate amount of time.

imPRESS

A static page description language used only on Imagen printers, imPRESS has capabilities roughly similar to those of PCL, including bit-mapped fonts, and the ability to combine commands into macros. In contrast to PCL, however, few software vendors have been enticed to write imPRESS drivers for their applications, and no other hardware companies have announced imPRESS printers. Font availability, in particular, is much poorer for imPRESS than for PCL.

With imPRESS, pages can be printed in any of four orientations. Graphics commands include rectangles, polygons, and elliptical and circular arcs. Shapes can be filled with a variety of patterns or shades, and bit maps can be reproduced at three levels of magnification.

To provide building blocks for generating text, imPRESS uses glyphs. One set of glyphs is permanently stored in the printer; more may be downloaded by an application. In addition to providing character shapes, glyphs are also used to provide patterns for filling graphics such as rectangles and ellipses.

Lasergraphics Package

An unusual approach to the page description problem is offered by Lasergraphics Corporation's Lasergraphics Package (LGP), currently available with the AST TurboLaser printer. Rather than functioning as a page description language, LGP coordinates the operations of four other languages built into the TurboLaser, each of which is optimized for a particular purpose. The first, Extended Diablo 630 emulation, provides control over text formatting comparable to PCL. The second, Extended Epson FX emulation, includes more rudimentary text capabilities, but provides compatibility with a range of MS-DOS graphics programs. The third, Lasergraphics Language, provides a number of operations for object graphics, including polygons and slices of pie charts. And the fourth, Hewlett-Packard Graphics Language emulation, allows the TurboLaser to be used with software applications originally written for plotters.

Two advantages of this approach are speed and compatibility. By knitting together several languages, each optimized for a particular type of printing, the printer can produce pages that combine text, graphics, and digitized images at a much higher speed than printers using a single page description language. In addition, because its Diablo, Epson, and HPGL emulations are supersets of popular printing protocols, the TurboLaser is immediately compatible with virtually all MS-DOS software.

The disadvantage of the LGP approach is its fragmentation, which does not allow the application of graphics transformations to text, as is possible under PostScript's generalized text/graphics model. The fact that LGP uses bit-mapped rather than outline fonts makes it less attractive than PostScript or DDL for applications with high typographic demands.

Chapter 11

Graphics

The term *graphics* covers a lot of ground, but at its simplest it means everything on a page that isn't text, including photographs, drawings, graphs, charts, patterns, and background tints. The definition can also be stretched to include rules and boxes, which in addition to their typographic roles can be used as graphic elements in their own right.

In the publishing and graphic arts industries, these elements have traditionally been bunched together under the label *artwork,* and they have typically been the labors of graphic artists. Computer systems play two distinct roles in printing graphics. The first is in creating line art or halftones; the second, in providing the means for bypassing traditional pasteup and directly combining artwork into documents. Although the entire process from creation of line art to final page makeup can take place on the computer, in practice you'll probably find that pragmatic and aesthetic considerations lead you to mix traditional and computerized methods. For example, some artwork is best prepared on a computer and some best prepared by hand; likewise, some images lend themselves to electronic pasteup while others should still be pasted in by hand. And why not? Even a cursory look back at the evolution of publishing will show a tendency of the trade to selectively adopt new technology while hanging on to old methods that remained superior. That practice makes just as much sense today.

As described in Chapter 2, two kinds of artwork are used for graphic reproduction: line art and halftones. Line art consists of only a single color and a background; halftones include intermediate shades. Line art doesn't necessarily have to be composed of lines, but all parts of the image must be composed of the same solid tone. An image created with a black felt-tip marker, for instance, is line art: there is only black and background, with no intermediate shades of gray.

In traditional publishing, line art is rendered as a *photostat* (or *line shot*) and pasted directly onto the page. When the line art is not fragile or valuable, the original artwork can often be pasted directly onto the mechanical. For creating line art via computer, the spectrum of software includes freehand drawing programs suitable for illustrators, business and scientific graphics programs providing pre-formatted charts and graphs for persons with no graphics training, and clip art, collections of ready-made pictures that represent the ultimate in automated illustration.

In addition to being divided according to the applications they serve, graphics programs can be further separated into *raster graphics* and *object graphics*. With raster graphics, there is a one-to-one correspondence between the pixels displayed on the computer monitor and the dots printed by the output device. The files created by such programs are matrices of zeros and ones.

The strength of the raster graphics approach is that it provides complete control over the appearance of an illustration. Usually such programs allow a portion of the screen to be enlarged so that individual pixels can be edited; for example, the *FatBits* mode popularized by Apple's MacPaint program. The disadvantage of raster graphics is that the images produced by the program are device dependent. Since the resolution of the display is much lower than that of the output device, curves and diagonal lines may have a jagged appearance when printed by a laser printer or a typesetting machine. Some programs, however, provide smoothing algorithms to mitigate the problem.

Programs that use the object graphics approach store illustrations in the form of mathematical descriptions of their constituent parts. This allows the file to be quite compact, dramatically reducing the time required to transmit it to the printer. More importantly, assuming the output device is capable of interpreting the mathematical description, the illustration can be printed at the full resolution available on the output device.

Computer-Generated Line Art

The simplest kind of line art—rules and boxes—is often the most effective. When enclosed in a 1-point box, an ordinary table gains a professional appearance. In the traditional sequence of creating a document, incorporation of such graphics generally takes place at pasteup time, since the size and location of rules and other simple graphics is closely tied to the arrangement of text on the page. The same applies to documents created via electronic means. Commands to create rules and other simple graphic elements should be part of the program you are using to lay out the page.

Unfortunately, if that program is a standard word processor, it probably lacks commands for creating simple graphics. In some cases, utilities—small, special-purpose programs—are available to provide a particular word processor with the capability to produce rules, boxes, and background shades.

Page makeup programs make it easier to create simple graphics. Typically, such applications allow you to select from a menu the type of graphic element you wish to use and then position it on the page using a mouse or by specifying its coordinates.

For generating more complex graphics, stand-alone programs are needed. The most popular of these are business and scientific graphics programs. By providing a variety of preformatted charts or graphs, this software allows those without special training to produce the sort of professional results that previously were the province of the graphic artist. Numerous programs are available for graphically depicting the results of statistical analyses or the contents of spreadsheets and databases.

Most such programs were developed for dot matrix printers or plotters, a heritage which may result in some difficulties in adapting them to the laser printer. In order to successfully exploit the full 300-dpi resolution of the typical laser printer, a new driver must be written for the program.

Typically, graphics programs include their own fonts used for labeling charts and graphs. Since these fonts were almost always designed originally for use with plotters and dot matrix printers, generally they produce lettering that is inferior to laser printer typefaces. Newer versions of graphics programs may let you use the laser printer's own fonts. Otherwise, for best results you should print the image without labels, generating these separately and combining them with the image using either a page makeup program or manual pasteup.

For general purpose illustration requirements, two types of drawing programs are available. One kind, which uses the raster approach, supports freehand drawing using a mouse, a graphics pad, or a joystick. The classic and much-imitated example is MacPaint, which allows you to zoom in to edit individual pixels; zoom out in order to view the entire page at once; pan around a "virtual canvas" that is larger than can be shown all at once on the screen; create shapes such as rectangles, ovals, and circles; move or stretch a portion of the picture; select patterns and shades of gray with which to fill arbitrary shapes; create custom fill patterns; and copy a portion of the picture to another location.

The second type of drawing program, which uses the object graphics approach, tends to provide a more structured and geometrically-oriented set of capabilities than programs that store their files in raster form. The capabilities for generating and printing geometrical shapes are more advanced than raster graphics drawing programs. In addition, some object graphics programs are beginning to allow freehand drawing. One major difference between the two types of drawing programs is the quality of their output on a laser printer. Raster graphics are printed at the resolution of the display—relatively low when compared to that available with a laser printer or typesetting machine. The telltale ragged edges of these graphics betray their origin on a computer. One way to get around that problem is to draw them at a much larger scale than you intend to print them. Another solution is a smoothing algorithm built into the application driver, which does just

Figure 11-1 Sample of clip art, from the Click Art Publications collection.

what its name implies—it smooths the jagged edges of curves and diagonal lines. Drawing programs that use the object approach, on the other hand, produce resolution-independent output files that are then rendered at the resolution of the output device.

Clip art traditionally referred to sets of fanciful or utilitarian drawings sold at art supply shops and used by graphic artists for routine purposes such as Yellow Pages ads. The existence of drawing programs for personal computers has provided another means for the dissemination of clip art—as files on a disk (see Figure 11-1). Clip art collections include not only illustrative drawings, but also maps and symbols. The advantage of computer clip art over traditional clip art is that once the illustration is brought into your drawing program, you can crop, scale, and edit it.

Prerecorded CD-ROM disks, which offer inexpensive mass data storage, are a promising means for distributing clip art collections. While a floppy disk can hold at most only several dozen picture files, a CD-ROM disk can hold several thousand. Advances in CD-ROM technology should spur the development of large clip art libraries for specialized uses.

Synthetic Halftones

In contrast to line art, which has only solid shades, the typical photograph or other halftone image has regions that vary from black to white with a broad spectrum of grays in between—this is called a *continuous-tone* (or *contone*) image. In traditional printing processes, photographs and other artwork containing shades of gray are photographed through an intermediate screen prior to printing to convert the shades into dots of various sizes; hence the term *screened art*. Breaking the continuous-tone image into dots is necessary because most presses cannot lay down shades of gray. The varying-sized dots create the illusion of gray despite the use of a single color of ink in the printing press. Note that in traditional screening, the number of dots in any given area remains constant; it is the size of the dots that is varied to produce relative color densities (see Figure 11-2).

As in digital type, the resolution of the screen is directly related to the clarity of the final image—the finer the dot pattern used by the screen, the more clearly the image can be rendered. Standard halftone densities are 65, 85, 100, 120, 133, and 150 screen dots per inch. The fineness of the line screen you choose for your halftones depends on the capabilities of the printer or typesetting machine you use and the paper you print on. In printing jargon, screens are usually spoken of in lines per inch. A 133-line screen, for instance, has 133 screen dots per inch horizontally and vertically.

Dot screen resolutions should not be confused with the higher resolution of laser printers and phototypesetting machines (300 dpi to 2500 dpi). Although a halftone resolution of 100 screen dots per inch may seem coarse in comparison,

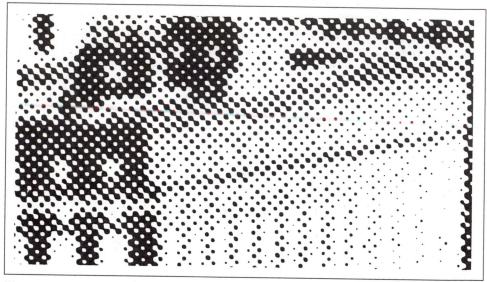

Figure 11-2 *A magnified view of a dot screen produced using the traditional method of photographing the image through an opaque screen.*

remember that within this fixed density of dots, the individual dots will range in size, depending on the shade of gray being produced. For example, to produce a five percent shade of gray with a 133-line screen, each individual dot is only about $1/600$ inch in diameter, which is close to the threshold of what is visible to the eye.

A close relative of the dot screen is the line screen. Here, the image is photographed through a grid of opaque parallel lines, resulting in lines that become thicker in darker areas and thinner in lighter areas.

In desktop publishing, several techniques are used to generate halftones. One method, called *randomizing,* prints dots in a random pattern that varies in density according to the shade of gray. This method is the opposite of the traditional screening process, in which the density of dots remains constant while the size of the individual dots changes to produce different shades. A second method, called *dithering,* produces the effect of wandering lines on the page, with the pattern becoming denser in darker parts of an image (Figure 11-3).

The third approach is simply to mimic a traditional screen. A problem with that method is that the dots printed by a laser printer are fixed in size; to simulate the varying-sized dots of the traditional dot screen, laser-printer dots are fused together into grains, as illustrated in Figure 11-4. The smallest possible grain is, of course, a single dot. Since each grain is formed by combining one or more dots, the size of the grains, and hence the darkness of the shade of gray being rendered, can

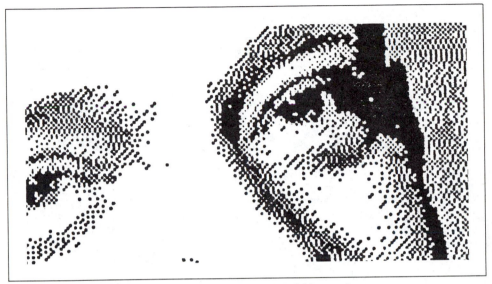

Figure 11-3 Magnified view of dithering, printed on a 300-dpi laser printer.

vary only in discrete steps. For example, suppose a laser printer is configured to print halftones using 16 levels of gray. This would be done by dividing the entire page into four-dot by four-dot cells. In each such cell the number of dots that can be combined into a grain ranges from 1 to 16. On a 300-dpi laser printer, this configuration is the equivalent of a 75-line halftone screen with 16 levels of gray. Such a screen approximately matches the coarseness of halftones used in newspapers, but many more levels of gray are available for newspaper printing. On the laser printer, the image is not only coarse, but the borders of gray shades may show up as noticeable contours.

With a 300-dpi laser printer, a tradeoff between resolution and *grayscale* (the number of gray levels) is unavoidable. It's possible to increase the grayscale, but only by reducing the resolution of the screen. For example, you can have 36 levels of gray by building each cell out of a 6-by-6 box of dots, but doing so lowers the resolution to a coarse 50 cells per inch. There's no way—short of switching to a higher resolution printing device—to get around this tradeoff.

The bottom line is that 300-dpi laser printers can't approach even the fairly low-grade halftones in your daily newspaper. For most applications, such as newsletters or technical reports, you're better off taking the photographs you wish to include in your document to a graphic arts shop for screening via traditional means, leaving a blank box in the document and pasting in the halftone prior to printing.

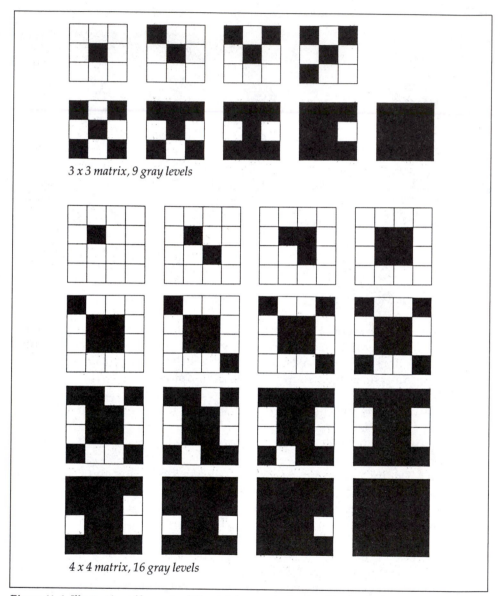

3 x 3 matrix, 9 gray levels

4 x 4 matrix, 16 gray levels

Figure 11-4 *Illustration of how a traditional dot screen is simulated by fusing laser printer dots together into grains of varying sizes. With grains built on a 3-by-3 matrix, 9 levels of gray are possible; with grains built on a 4-by-4 matrix, the printer can produce 16 levels. (Courtesy of Personal Publishing)*

So far, our discussion of how halftones are rendered on a laser printer has ignored the question of how an image is digitized in the first place and converted into a form that the laser printer can print. As described in Chapter 8, you can use a scanner to convert an image into digital form. Once it is converted, the resulting grid of grayscale values is ready to be processed at three locations—by the scanner's own software, by graphics programs running on a personal computer, and by the raster image processor of the laser printer.

Depending on the scanner model, the scanner's own software may provide controls for any or all of the following: contrast, brightness, cropping, and type of dithering pattern. After finishing this first stage of processing, many scanners store the image as a computer file in a format usable by a personal computer graphics program. Many graphics programs allow images to be cropped or edited pixel by pixel. Particularly in the case of halftones generated by low-resolution digitizers, the ability to edit the picture is useful for cleaning up jagged edges or altering the intensity of gray in a poorly lit part of the picture.

Naturally, the possibilities of digital picture editing are endless. Feel like proving the existence of flying saucers? Want to "document" a quorum by inserting absent board members into their usual seats? While these examples may seem far-fetched, digital picture editing has actually been used widely for several years on expensive dedicated image-processing systems. Most famous is the case of the *National Geographic* magazine "moving" one of the three Great Pyramids of Giza to fit it into a cover photograph. Now, for desktop-published materials as well, seeing is no longer believing.

The final stage of editing, which occurs within the laser printer, is only possible if the printer is equipped with a page description language that provides commands for digital image manipulation. With such a printer, data can be transmitted as a grid of grayscale values. Then you can determine the appearance of the synthetic halftone by specifying the number of shades of gray to be printed as well as the angle of the screen.

Other sorts of manipulations are also possible. Instead of a dot screen, you can use a line screen, which renders shades of gray by printing lines of varying thickness. You can also reverse black and white to create a negative and alter the contrast or brightness of the image. For example, to increase contrast, all values of gray recorded by the digitizer below a given level are reduced and all above that level are increased.

Even with such manipulations, halftone output on a laser printer is still lower in quality than traditional screened art. PostScript's device independence, however, allows you to use the laser printer for proofing and then produce final output on a PostScript-compatible typesetting machine. With this combination of equipment, a desktop publishing system can actually produce a broad range of special halftone effects much more easily than would be possible with traditional methods. Figures 11-5 and 11-6, produced using an ImagiTex 1085 scanner, a Macintosh,

Graphics

Figure 11-5 At left, a scanned photograph of San Francisco's Transamerica Tower, printed on a 2540-dpi Linotron 300 phototypesetting machine using PostScript's default halftone settings a 90-line dot screen at a 45-degree screen angle. At right, a 20-line dot screen at a 45-degree angle.

and a 2540-dpi Linotronic 300 phototypesetting machine, show some possible manipulations of a single photograph.

A final consideration for digital halftones is reproducibility, but the factors that may cause an image to reproduce well or poorly are not easy to isolate. A pair of halftones produced by two different laser printers may appear equal in quality, but one may reproduce well with an offset process while the other may not, for reasons related to the shape, clarity, and uniformity of the halftone dots. If you are buying a printer to create masters for offset printing, examine a document printed using that printer or one with the same type of engine.

136

Figure 11-6 *The high-contrast image on the left is created by setting a threshold level of gray. Any shade darker than the threshold level is printed as black; any shade lighter than the threshold, as white. On the right, a contoured effect is created by setting the number of gray levels at four.*

Graphics Monitors

Any graphics software package is only as powerful as the computer monitor used with it, since the monitor provides the working surface for interactively creating and altering an image. Computer monitors are of three types: character, vector, and raster. Character monitors have a particular font "hard-wired" into the system, that is, the font is stored permanently in the read-only memory of the monitor. Limiting the capabilities of the monitor to this screen font allows the monitor's performance to be optimized for sharp representation of characters and for avoiding undesirable effects such as flicker. Simple rule and box graphics can be displayed on such monitors, since the character set built into the screen typically includes some simple graphics characters, allowing borders or shaded areas to be displayed. More complex graphics require a true graphics monitor.

Vector monitors are not commonly used with personal computers, except in some specialized engineering and architecture workstations. Just as a character monitor is optimized for text, a vector monitor is optimized for line graphics; built into the monitor is a set of commands for drawing lines, shaded areas, circles, and other graphic shapes. With these commands, a software application can quickly and efficiently generate and modify complex images, making vector monitors ideally suited for such demanding uses as animation and three-dimensional wireframe engineering design. Conversely, the vector monitor is an awkward vehicle for text, which it displays using "stick figure" characters.

Raster monitors are by far the most common type of monitor used with personal computer graphics programs. In these, each pixel shown by the monitor is controlled by a digital bit in the computer's memory, making the raster monitor the visual analog of the laser printer. In contrast to the parochialism of the character and vector monitors, the raster monitor has no particular bent toward either text or graphics. It is well-suited for handling either or both at the same time.

That flexibility has a flip side. Without a screen font hard-wired into the monitor, a great deal more data must be conveyed from the computer in order to display a passage of text. To display a Z on a character monitor, for example, the computer merely sends the code number assigned to that character in the screen font. But to display a Z on a raster monitor, the computer must send the status of each of the hundred or so pixels that make up the matrix on which the letter is drawn. To compensate for the greater amount of data that must be transferred for each letter, raster monitors generally show text at somewhat lower resolution than character-oriented monitors. For example, in the screen font used by the IBM Monochrome Monitor, a character monitor, each character is built on a 9-pixel by 14-pixel grid; the IBM Color Graphics Monitor, a raster monitor, uses a coarser 8-pixel by 8-pixel grid. While legible, text shown at lower resolution is too hard on the eyes to be suitable for prolonged text processing. When considering the purchase of a monitor, the question should not be, "Can I read this?" Rather, you should ask, "Can I read this comfortably for hours at a time?"

Another issue to consider is the relation between the way text and graphics appear on the monitor and the way they look when finally printed. Even the best monitors, those capable of displaying sharp graphic images, have much lower resolution than laser printers and phototypesetting machines. For example, at 72 pixels per inch (5184 per square inch), the density of pixels on the Macintosh screen is less than six percent of the density printed by the typical laser printer, with its 300-dpi (90,000 dots per square inch) resolution.

Why the drastic difference? One reason is the fact that the laser printers must be able to print a page every seven to ten seconds, while a monitor must "print" the entire display at the rate of about 60 times each second in order to avoid noticeable screen flicker. A recent innovation is the "proofing monitor," so called because it is updated every several seconds and thus is not usable for interactive word processing or document formatting. Such a monitor, which offers very high resolution (in the 150-dpi range) is designed to be used side by side with a standard monitor to provide a WYSIWYG image of the printed page.

Because of the inevitable difference in resolution between the standard graphics monitor and the printed page, there are some things about the printed document that your monitor simply can't tell you. It can't accurately show you shades of gray, precise distances between letters and between lines, and typefaces at small sizes. In addition, some monitors use rectangular rather than square pixels, distorting the aspect ratio—the relation between the vertical and horizontal dimensions—of an image. Currently, the best graphics displays have about 1 million pixels, while a more typical number is about 250,000. Compare that to the 9 million spots printed on a page by a 300-dpi laser printer or the 400 million spots printed by a 2000-dpi phototypesetter. At best the ratio is about 9 printed spots per screen pixel; at worst, about 1600 printed spots per screen pixel. Because of this difference, typefaces cannot be rendered accurately on the screen, especially at small point sizes, nor can the distance between pairs of letters. Thus, on-screen kerning is ruled out, at least for small point sizes, unless the software provides a magnifying glass feature that gives you the opportunity to scan a blown-up version of your text. But even that option is not a perfect solution, since the only way to see if the spacing in a letter pair must be adjusted is to see text at its normal size. For this reason, the WYSIWYG ideal of a perfect match between monitor and printed output is just that: an ideal. That's not to say WYSIWYG is a useless concept; only that it has definite limits given current technology.

A chronic difficulty for those assembling a desktop publishing system is the prevailing lack of standardization in graphics hardware. Macintosh users are fortunate in this regard, since all models of that computer use the same raster monitor. The IBM PC, however, is the locus of several conflicting graphics standards. Options include the IBM Color Graphics Adapter (640 by 200 pixels maximum, or about 80 pixels horizontally and 35 pixels vertically per inch); the IBM Enhanced Graphics Adapter (640 by 350 pixels, or about 80 by 55 pixels per inch); the Hercules graphics board (720 by 348 pixels, or 90 by 63 pixels per inch when attached to a standard monochrome monitor); and various high-cost, high-resolution monitors.

The existence of multiple graphics standards can make it difficult to find hardware that can be used with all the applications software you want to combine in your desktop publishing system. The problem is especially acute for those who want to combine the output of several graphics and text programs via page make-up software. But two developments offer hope to ease the problems caused by conflicting standards. One is the increasing tendency for new graphics boards and monitors to offer multiple modes, including the older standards. This provides "upward compatibility," allowing you to benefit from new technology without sacrificing older applications to obsolescence.

The other potential solution is the arrival of "smart screens" with built-in graphics coprocessor chips for enhanced performance and a standard screen description language. With such a language mediating between the application and the screen, programs need only produce a high-level description of the screen; the screen description language then handles the details of rendering the screen. An example of such a language is QuickDraw, the set of graphics routines built into the Macintosh computer. Unfortunately, the code underlying QuickDraw is not licensed by Apple to other graphics monitor makers, and thus does not have the potential to become an industry standard. Such interface standards have been proposed, but adoption has been slow due mainly to resistance from software developers, who are unwilling to accept the toll on speed exacted when an intermediate level of software is present between the application and the monitor. With a graphics coprocessor built into the monitor, a screen description language can be used without a reduction in performance. If this approach becomes common in monitor design, personal computer programs will be able to produce faster and more sophisticated graphics on the monitor.

Chapter 12

Assembling a Desktop Publishing System

Creating a useful desktop publishing system means combining a variety of hardware and software products and mastering a set of traditional and computer-age skills. In other chapters of this book you've looked at individual pieces of the puzzle. Now it's time to see how those parts combine to make a working system.

You don't have to be a computer expert to put together a desktop publishing system. It's more important to have a clear picture of the results you want than to have specific knowledge about equipment. Start with the documents you plan to publish, then work backward to the tools needed to create them.

The first factor to consider in planning a desktop publishing system is the complexity of the pages in the documents you plan to produce. The spectrum ranges from single-column, text-only pages to layouts that freely combine text, boxes, shaded regions, computer-generated graphics, and digitized photographs. Page complexity has numerous ramifications not only for software, but for hardware.

With each step upward in page complexity comes a parallel growth in the number of software packages required, as well as the amount of sophisticated hardware that must be marshalled for the task. For example, an entire novel can almost always be typeset using a single program, although if that program is to provide top-quality fonts and full typographic capabilities it may be very expensive. But to create a four-page business report that includes an occasional graph merged into a text page probably requires three programs: a word processing program to create the text, a business graphics program to create the chart, and a page makeup program to knit the two together.

Complex pages also require more sophisticated hardware: a more powerful computer, a high-resolution monitor and a mouse or a touchpad for graphics, and a scanner for digitized images. For documents that include only text, a complete desktop publishing system—including computer, laser printer, and software—can be assembled for less than $5000. For documents that also include pictures and scanned images, the typical system would almost certainly cost more than $10,000, due to the additional software and hardware required, as well as the fact that the computer must be a good deal more powerful (hence more expensive).

Another important factor is whether final output will be from a typesetting machine or a laser printer. If you intend to output to a typesetting machine, your software should have sophisticated typographic capabilities, especially those governing white space control, such as kerning and tracking. To set typographically inferior type on a typesetting machine is like giving an old car a new paint job without hammering out and smoothing the bumps and dents. The high gloss can't hide the crumminess underneath—in fact, it may serve to highlight it.

Typographic Features

Regardless of whether it is designed to handle simple pages or complex layouts combining words and illustrations, any desktop publishing system is only as good as its ability to handle text. Before desktop laser printers were in use, text-handling systems fell into two distinct categories—those driving a standard impact printer and those used with typesetting machines. The laser printer changed all that, setting up numerous lines of typographic latitude between the two poles of typed and typeset.

Word processing programs mark the low end of typographic control. Most word processing programs were designed before the arrival of laser printers and hence lacked many essential typographic features, such as allowing multiple typefaces within a document, handling proportionally spaced typographic fonts, and supporting adjustable leading. Newer releases of some of the more sophisticated word processors are beginning to provide such features, but their overall capabilities are still beneath the low end of true typesetting programs.

Beyond the capabilities of word processing, desktop publishing systems may provide a variety of typographic features. For simplicity's sake, we've divided them below into three levels: minimum, better, and better-yet.

The Minimum Configuration   In our minimum configuration, we've opted for tracking control rather than automatic kerning as a means of controlling the spacing of letters. This is simply because tracking is much easier to accomplish and hence more apt to be included in an inexpensive program. By using the tracking facility to tighten or loosen the overall letter spacing, you can achieve the visual effect of kerning for many letter combinations. By using the tracking facility to make the type very tight or very loose, you can make the letter spacing appear more even, obscuring the need for many minor kerning adjustments. This is not great typography, but it can greatly enhance the look of type produced on an inexpensive system.

For this minimum configuration, we have, however, included the ability to kern manually. This is mainly for the sake of your display type—the larger, headline-style type from about 16 points and up. In these sizes, bad letter spacing stands out like a sore thumb, and you really do need some remedy for troublesome letter combinations.

The minimum:
- tracking control
- manual kerning
- automatic hyphenation
- line leading in 1-point increments
- full quadding control
- horizontal rules
- variety of fixed spaces
- expandable hyphenation dictionary

A Better System   A better system takes the minimum standards one level higher. It offers automatic kerning instead of manual, with at least several hundred kerning pairs per typeface; a larger hyphenation dictionary based on roots or whole words with a logic-based backup hyphenation system; target ranges for letter spacing, to assist in aesthetically sound justified type; likewise, target ranges for spaceband widths, specifiable as maximum, minimum, and optimum values; the ability to add discretionary hyphens, to assist the hyphenation program with difficult or unfamiliar words; the ability to set vertical rules, which allows you to create ruled boxes and grids; and automatic indention codes that can be triggered by paragraph commands.

A better system:
- true hyphenation and justification program
- scalable fonts
- automatic kerning
- letter spacing ranges
- line leading in half-point increments
- spaceband control
- true, hard-margin tabs
- reverse and extra leading

- discretionary hyphens
- vertical rules
- automatic fraction building

The Better-Yet System   The better-yet system is at the threshold of a true commercial system, although we don't emphasize the speed that is a prerequisite for profitable professional typesetting. You can have a perfectly functional and practical typesetting system without the blazing speed of the professional models. In all likelihood, though, any system that includes all of the features we are outlining here is probably going to be pretty fast as well.

At this level, you should have at your command a full range of indention commands that can be used in conjunction with one another. You should have the ability to set type anywhere on the page with pin-point control using point markers and position commands. The h&j program should have a measured mode, allowing you to see on screen precisely how your type will be set. You should be able to drive several commercial typesetting machines, as well as being able to output to a laser printer. And with the ability to drive a typesetting machine, you should have excellent kerning control, with at least 1000 kern pairs per typeface.

At this level, you should also expect elaborate formatting capabilities, with multipart and nested formats as well as formats that can be linked to specific files or to all jobs on the system. This list selects only some of what we consider to be the major features of a top-notch typesetting system, the ones we feel are among the more important to look for when selecting a system.

The better-yet system:
- measured h&j facility
- point-marker coding
- skews and counting indents
- changeable character widths
- x-y coordinate positioning
- ability to output to several typesetting machines
- multipart and nested formats
- logical hyphen flags
- automatic fraction building
- horizontal escapement control
- alternate dictionaries

Pagination Features

While typographic controls apply to letter, word, line, and paragraph formatting, pagination or page makeup relates to the arrangement of text and graphics into pages. It includes such features as vertical column positioning, page numbering, generation of indexes and tables of contents, footnotes, placement of graphics, and flowing text from one page to the next.

As described in Chapter 2, software systems use either of two basic methods, interactive pagination or batch pagination, to accomplish the task of page makeup. With interactive page makeup programs, each graphic or text element is individually positioned on the page. With batch pagination programs, the entire document is automatically laid out according to formatting commands embedded in or attached to the document. Naturally, the two ways of working each have their own strengths and weaknesses.

Consider the difference between a brochure and a novel. In the case of the brochure, each page is unique and must be individually laid out. For this purpose, an interactive page makeup program that provides a WYSIWYG interface is perfectly suited because of the freedom it provides to freely position elements on the page. In the case of the novel, individually creating each page would not only be tedious, but could lead to inconsistencies in formatting within the document. For such an application, batch pagination provides a way of automatically applying a set of uniform formatting guidelines to a large number of pages.

The batch approach versus the interactive approach (and the WYSIWYG versus the non-WYSIWYG interface) are not distinct categories of software. Both ways of working may be provided within a single program. For example, a powerful approach is for a program to allow a set of master page layouts to be set up and viewed in an interactive, WYSIWYG fashion, with these layouts then automatically applied to the entire document in a batch fashion.

A variety of features are included in a full-featured set of pagination controls. One group of features act as constraints, automatically preventing unaesthetic layouts. For example widow and orphan control prevent the last line of a paragraph from appearing alone at the top of a page or column (a widow) or the first line of a paragraph from appearing at the bottom of a page or column (an orphan). Likewise, subheadings can be automatically prevented from being isolated at the bottom of a page.

Another group of features controls the formatting and placement of material, including that repeated at the top of every page (headers) and at the bottom of every page (footers). Typically, either the header or the footer will incorporate a page number, whose format (roman numerals, arabic numerals, etc.) can also be specified. Footnotes may also appear at the foot of the page, and the pagination program must allow long footnotes to flow to the following page. Some programs are capable of automatically placing illustrations and captions on the same page in which they are referenced.

For creating a balanced page appearance, pagination features include vertical justification or feathering, which adjusts line leading to fill out the page in the vertical dimension, and column balancing, which makes sure that on the final page of a chapter in a two column layout the two columns will be the same length. Finally, pagination features may allow the insertion of graphics, such as rules and boxes, at predefined locations. This feature is particularly important in documents with many figure references and footnotes, where these elements should automatically be placed on the page where they are referenced.

Unillustrated Documents

Word Processors

Until quite recently, the development of word processing software for personal computers has been skewed toward providing increasingly sophisticated editing features rather than typographic capabilities, a situation that reflected the limits of the dot matrix and daisy-wheel printers used with personal computers. After the arrival of laser printers, more sophisticated typographic and pagination features were appended to many word processors via add-on utility programs or new releases, but these retrofitted word processing programs have their own problems. If you're looking into a desktop publishing system that is an enhanced version of a word processor, you have to do more than merely consider what features the system provides; more important is how well the enhanced formatting capabilities are implemented. In many cases, supposedly powerful systems that are extensions of word processing programs are simply too awkward and unreliable to serve as practical tools.

As described in Chapter 5, word processors use three different methods for formatting: embedded codes, formatting by menus, and formatting by style sheets. For popular word processing programs such as WordStar, utilities have been created that work in conjunction with the word processor to provide additional typographic and graphic functions. With such a program, you use the word processor in your accustomed manner for entering and editing text. In addition, you insert commands into the file that are recognized by the utility. In some cases you can then proceed to print the document in the normal fashion. With other programs, the utility adds an additional step to the printing process.

The problem with using a utility is the awkwardness involved in adding special codes to a document and using a separate program for printing. Cluttered with codes, the text becomes difficult to format correctly. Changing particular formatting elements, such as moving the location of a page break or changing the typeface used for subheads, requires that you painstakingly reedit the special formatting commands. For the coding method to be practical, the word processor must have the ability to apply its search-and-replace operation to embedded codes; unfortunately, many word processors lack this critical function.

In addition to formatting problems are performance issues. Utilities tend to be slow, and because they are separate programs, the word processor and the utility may not dovetail smoothly; in fact, they may interact in unpredictable ways, leading to bugs.

Finally, most formatting utilities do not really remedy the fact that programs like WordStar and MultiMate were not designed to handle the character-spacing adjustments necessary for proper formatting of proportional fonts. True typographic control of letter spacing and word spacing is beyond their capabilities. For example, to justify text set in a proportional typeface, the typical approach used by a utility is to add additional spaces between words, resulting in an excessively airy look. A slightly better solution is a word processor that has been internally revised to support one or more laser printers. Often, a vendor will take a regular word processor, enhance the printing module, and reissue it as a "desktop publishing" program. Unfortunately, this approach results in most of the same drawbacks as utilities, for the simple reason that formatting capabilities have been slapped on top of software that was not originally designed for such features.

To really provide adequate support for a laser printer, a word processor has to be designed from the ground up with the appropriate formatting and type-handling capabilities. In general, such programs use the style-sheet method of formatting, which merely requires that you label each element of text with a brief code signifying the appropriate format. The codes themselves do not specify the particular formatting operations that are attached to them—they indicate only what type of text element is being labeled. The formatting details invoked by the codes are specified in the style sheet, a separate computer file.

An example of successful implementation of this approach is Microsoft Word. With Word, formatting is done by labeling each document element with a two-letter code: SP, standard paragraph; S1, level-one subhead; FN, footnote; and so on. The formats defined in the style sheet for each code can be applied to any block of text, from a single character to the document as a whole.

Once created, a Word style sheet can be applied to any document. Conversely, different style sheets can be attached to the same document. For example, with style sheet A, technical writers could print drafts of a document on an inexpensive laser printer, such as the Hewlett-Packard LaserJet. Later, the production department staff could attach style sheet B, containing formats for the Apple LaserWriter printer.

The method allows complex formats to be applied to a document without impairing the program's ease of use for editing. Another advantage is that it encourages the application of a consistent design. Most importantly, being able to name formats and save them allows for global changes—alterations that affect the document as a whole. For example, if you have labeled all subheads with the subhead tag and you later decide to have them all appear in a different typeface than

DIGEST OF PUBLIC GENERAL BILLS AND RESOLUTIONS

H.R. 1236 MR. ROBERTS; 1/4/77

Repeals the Postal Reorganization Act. Reenacts provisions relating to the postal service which were in effect immediately prior to the enactment of such Act.

```
1   DI Division 1                             STANDARD DIVISION
       Page break. Page length 11"; width 8.5". Page # format Arabic. Top
       margin 1"; bottom 1"; left 1.25"; right 3.5". Top running head at
       0.5". Bottom running head at 0.5". Footnotes on same page.
2   TX Paragraph 3                            STANDARD TEXT
       TMSRMN (roman i) 10/12. Justified.
3   SH Paragraph 2                            SUBHEAD
       TMSRMN (roman i) 10/12 Bold Uppercase. Flush left, space before 10
       pt.
4   TI Paragraph 1                            TITLE
       TMSRMN (roman i) 12 Bold Uppercase. Centered.
```

DIGEST OF PUBLIC GENERAL BILLS AND RESOLUTIONS

H.R. 1236 Mr. Roberts; 1/4/77

Repeals the Postal Reorganization Act. Reenacts provisions relating to the postal service which were in effect immediately prior to the enactment of such Act.

```
1   DI Division 1                             STANDARD DIVISION
       Page break. Page length 11"; width 8.5". Page # format Arabic. Top
       margin 1"; bottom 1"; left 1.25"; right 3.3". Top running head at
       0.5". Bottom running head at 0.5". Footnotes on same page.
2   TX Paragraph 3                            STANDARD TEXT
       HELV (modern i) 10/12. Justified (first line indent 0.3").
3   SH Paragraph 2                            SUBHEAD
       HELV (modern i) 10/12 Bold Underlined. Centered, space before 1 li.
4   TI Paragraph 1                            TITLE
       HELV (modern i) 12 Bold Small caps. Flush left.
```

Figure 12-1 *By making minor changes in a Microsoft Word style sheet, you can make global changes in a document. The two documents shown here were produced from identical text files; the differences in formatting between the two are the result of differences in the two attached style sheets.*

you originally intended, you need to make only one change—in the style sheet—rather than change each individual subhead. Figure 12-1 shows two versions of a document and the style sheets used to create them; the differences between the two are the result of the three changes indicated in the second style sheet.

Professional Composition Systems

Beyond the functionality of word processing software are more powerful typesetting and batch pagination programs. Some have been developed specifically for laser printers, while others are adaptations of software originally used to drive phototypesetting machines. Some are designed to produce galleys for manual pasteup, and these lack pagination features such as indexes, footnotes, and page formatting. In most cases, professional composition programs can drive not only a desktop laser printer, but also at least one kind of phototypesetting machine, in which case the desktop printer may be used for proofing and previewing text that will later be set on a more sophisticated machine, as well as for producing low-resolution final output.

The pricing of document-processing software shows the collision between two markets—the personal computer software market, in which most software is traditionally priced below a thousand dollars, and the typesetting market, where prices range into the tens of thousands. Typesetting system vendors introducing versions of their products for personal computers have been forced to make drastic cuts in order to compete, but the prices are still astronomical by personal computer standards, ranging to $10,000. The best, however, equal the functionality of minicomputer-based phototypesetter front ends.

This book was typeset using a program in this category—Magna Computer Systems' MagnaType, an implementation of the popular Computer Composition International (CCI) commercial typographic system. It runs on the IBM PC and drives PostScript-equipped laser printers and a variety of typesetting machines.

Prior to formatting by MagnaType, the appropriate mnemonic formatting codes are embedded in text using a word processor or MagnaType's own text editor. One significant feature of the program is the ability to create customized generic codes for particular formats. These codes can then be associated with one set of formatting instructions in one document, and with another set of formatting instructions in another document. For example, SS1 can be used as the code for a first-level subhead; in one document it can refer to centered Helvetica, in another to flush-left, bold Palatino. Another significant feature of MagnaType is its support for a limited form of multitasking, which allows you to begin reviewing hyphenation and justification at the beginning of a document while the h&j routine processes the remainder of the file.

$$\left(\int_{-\infty}^\infty e^{-x^2} \,dx \right)^2 = \pi$$

$$\begin{pmatrix} a_{11} & a_{12} & \cdots & a_{1n} \\ a_{21} & a_{22} & \cdots & a_{2n} \\ \vdots & \vdots & \ddots & \vdots \\ a_{m1} & a_{m2} & \cdots & a_{mn} \end{pmatrix}$$

$$\sum_{l \text{ odd}} \binom{n}{l} = 2^{n-1}$$

```
$$\left( \int_{-\infty}^\infty e^{-x^2} \,dx\right)^2 =\pi$$
$$\pmatrix a_{11} & a_{12} & \hdots & a_{1n} \\
          a_{21} & a_{22} & \hdots & a_{2n} \\
          \vdots & \vdots & \ddots & \vdots \\
          a_{m1} & a_{m2} & \hdots & a_{mn} \endpmatrix$$
$$\sum_{\text{$l$ odd}}\binom nl=2^{n-1}$$
```

Figure 12-2 A formula typeset with TeX and the macros used to produce it.

While most high-level typesetting packages, such as MagnaType, are adaptations of dedicated systems, a significant exception is TeX. Although it can produce results comparable to commercial typesetting and batch pagination systems, TeX was devised outside the commercial typesetting world in response to the demands associated with setting formulas in mathematical and scientific documents. It is built around a unique set of formatting concepts derived from the methods traditionally used to set type by hand. Elements of text, from individual letters to complex equations, can be defined as boxes. The language then provides a method for joining such boxes together to form pages.

TeX, which is now available for Macintoshes and PC-compatible microcomputers, provides several hundred basic commands, known as primitives. It allows additional commands, called macros, to be created from these primitives, and libraries of such commands are readily available with the software packages and from TeX user groups. Figure 12-2 shows a formula typeset using TeX and the set of macros used to specify its formatting.

As with traditional typesetting systems, TeX files are created with a word processor, with which you embed the necessary commands. Unlike many commercial typesetting systems, the program does not depend on any special keyboard keys and hence can be used with any personal computer. Once the file has been created, TeX composes it. At least one personal computer implementation provides a WYSIWYG screen preview of the final page, but to make changes you must edit the original file.

Hardware for Text-Only Systems

Generally speaking, creation of text-only documents places relatively modest demands on the computer system, in contrast to the more sophisticated systems necessary when graphics and digitized images are merged with text. Normally, an unenhanced IBM PC or compatible computer is sufficient. The programs that emulate commercial typesetting and batch pagination systems, however, often require a more powerful microcomputer than a standard PC in order to achieve acceptable speed, particularly for hyphenation routines. The MS-DOS operating system of such computers is single-tasking, meaning that the computer can work with only one program at a time.

The type of laser printer appropriate for text-only documents varies according to the demands of the document. For fairly simple office documents, you may find that one of the more inexpensive laser printers with sets of fonts on ROM cartridges may suffice. Printers used for text-only applications do not require the megabyte or more of memory necessary for full-page graphics printing.

For most applications, a laser printer that can handle downloadable fonts is desirable, since it allows a more flexible choice of different typefaces and sizes. Obviously, a laser printer that stores fonts as outlines rather than bit maps provides more flexibility in choice of sizes. And for printers used as proofing devices for phototypesetting systems, the same set of fonts should be available for the printer as for the phototypesetting machine. Generally, text-only documents can be handled adequately by printers that incorporate a static page description language, since the powers of dynamic languages to rotate type and perform other text acrobatics are not called for.

Illustrated Documents

The addition of graphics to the printed page makes the pagination process a good deal more complex. The greater the number and variety of graphics that must be incorporated with text, the less well the batch pagination approach serves the purpose and the more attractive the capabilities of interactive page makeup features.

Software for Merging Text and Graphics

The simplest example of the batch pagination approach to merging text and graphics are utility programs that allow graphics to be inserted into documents printed by word processing programs. Typically, such utilities are RAM resident, that is, they are loaded into the computer's memory but are inactive until called up. After creating a graphic image using a graphics program, you can invoke the utility to clip the boundaries of the picture and save it in a file. Later, you insert the name of the graphic image file at the appropriate location in your text file. The utility handles the task of merging the two files when the file is printed. Figure 12-3 shows a page created with this approach.

The problem with this simple method of merging text and graphics is that the utility does not handle the entire task of readjusting the text to make room for the image. Usually, such utilities will merely move the text down the page a sufficient distance to make room for the graphic, but they are not capable of reformatting the text to flow around the graphic. In addition, it is difficult to adjust the size, cropping, and position of the image being inserted into text.

The key element in interactive page makeup programs is the WYSIWYG working surface, which allows various arrangements of text, graphics, and images to be tried out, and which allows all elements on the page to be freely moved about. Usually, the program emulates the graphic artist's pasteup table, with a blank working surface and tools represented in a menu alongside, representing operations such as cutting and pasting.

Some programs use an entirely interactive approach, meaning that every element of text or graphics is individually positioned and formatted on the page. These generally limit you to working only on a single page at a time. Other programs use a combination of the interactive and the batch pagination approach. For example, with Xerox's Ventura Publisher, shown in Figure 12-4, text is formatted by labeling each element, such as a caption or a first-level subhead, with a "tag." Each tag contains all the formatting information associated with that element, such as font and leading. When you alter the definition of a tag, the program globally reformats all elements of the document that have been labeled with that tag, a batch pagination approach. On the other hand, the screen always provides a WYSIWYG view of the page, making the program highly interactive.

The demands of page makeup programs dovetail neatly with the features of the Macintosh and other computers using a similar user interface—the ability to show text and graphics as they will appear (or reasonably close to the way they will appear) on the printed page, the use of the mouse for positioning elements, the

Information Sheet #6
West Pines Spinal Clinic
J.M. Dundee, R.P.T.

Back Injuries and Activities

Many students at Back School have asked why some activities seem to place more stress on their backs than others. This chart provides at least a partial explanation. It shows how the pressure on the L3 disc varies in response to different positions. As you can see from the chart, standing erect places more than twice as much pressure on the disc as lying down. Walking places more pressure on the disc than standing erect, and sitting places more pressure than walking. Laughing raises the pressure above sitting, but only temporarily.

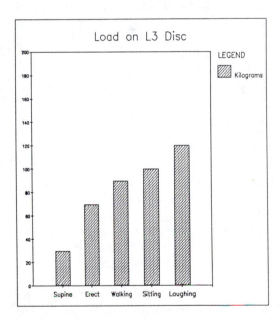

The data is from Buerger and Tabis (eds.), *Approaches to the Validation of Manipulation Therapy*. Charles C. Thomas, Springfield, IL, 1977.

Figure 12-3 *This page, showing the integration of a chart into a text page, was created with Microsoft Word and the Ram-Resident PrintMerge utility.*

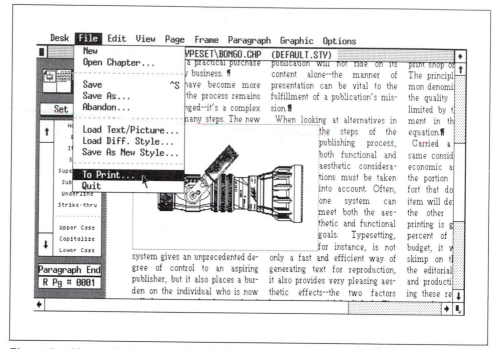

Figure 12-4 Ventura Publisher combines the batch and interactive approaches to document formatting. The menu on the left shows a list of tags, each storing font, leading, and other formatting information. When a tag is redefined, the entire document automatically reformats itself. At the same time, the WYSIWYG view of the document allows the effect of the formatting to be instantly viewed, a feature shared by interactive page makeup programs.

use of windows to assist cutting and pasting from one program into another, and the standardized menu system that makes it easy to move in and out of different programs without learning a new set of commands. Figure 12-5 shows Aldus's PageMaker program, the most popular page makeup program developed so far. Since page makeup software is still growing up fast, it is impossible to define the characteristics of low-end versus high-end. The following, however, are some important features to consider in picking a program.

Native and Imported Graphics Any page makeup program should provide a variety of easy-to-use tools for creating graphics such as rules, boxes, shaded areas, and patterns. You should be able to adjust the dimensions of imported graphics to fit within a specified box.

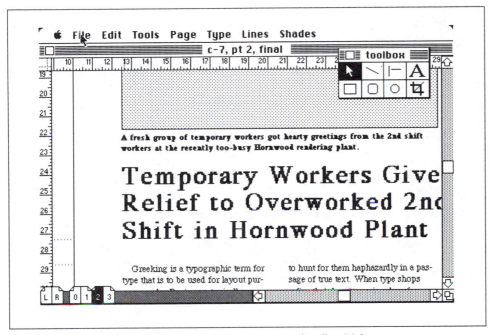

Figure 12-5 *Typically, interactive page makeup programs such as PageMaker are designed to resemble a graphic artist's workbench. Commands are invoked and elements are positioned using a mouse.*

Functions selected from the icons in the toolbox allow clipping, entry of text, and creation of rules, boxes, and circles. The menu bar at the top provides addition commands for handling files, editing, and formatting the page. Placement grids can be drawn onto the page using rulers along the side.

Text Editing   Although most page makeup programs are not designed to replace your standard word processor, most do provide an internal text editor to allow revisions and corrections to be made without exiting the program. Steer clear of any program that doesn't provide at least a rudimentary editor; text changes need to be made frequently enough that exiting the program simply to make one or two minor text changes soon becomes intolerably time-consuming. With some programs, text changes made within the page makeup program are not stored in the original text file. This can create extra work if the file must be updated or if constituent files edited within it need to be used again.

Typographic Features   Page makeup programs are gradually incorporating additional typographic features such as automatically shaping text around graphics or within predefined outlines, hyphenation and justification, kerning, tracking control, and vertical space control. Unfortunately, such features will exact an inevitable toll in the speed of the program.

Pagination   As noted above, programs differ in the degree to which they lean toward a batch or an interactive approach. Obviously, those with batch formatting capabilities are more suitable for longer documents. An important feature here is the ability to confine rippling to a given page or set of pages. That way, a small typographic error found on an early page might be corrected at a late stage in production without having to reprint all subsequent pages of a long document.

Compatibility   The page makeup program is, in effect, the hub of the desktop publishing system, joining text from word processors, computer graphics from drawing and chart-making programs, clip art from libraries of illustrations, and scanned images from digitizing systems. This makes compatibility a prime consideration in choosing a page makeup program. Most organizations have settled on a particular word processor as a standard. For document production to be efficient, the program being used for formatting and printing the document should be able to recognize and incorporate any formatting—such as boldfacing, italics, indents, and tabs—that was done to the document while it was being word processed. Otherwise, all formatting has to be redone from scratch.

Direct Control of the Printer   For special features such as performing a graphics operation on a large, outlined character, a desirable feature is the ability to insert page description language commands into the text file. Even more convenient are utilities that allow you to select special effects from a menu, eliminating the need for you to acquire proficiency in using the page description language.

Hardware for Illustrated Document Systems

As noted at the beginning of this chapter, creation of a complex document may require knitting together five or more different programs: one for drawings, one for charts, one for text editing, one for halftone images, and one for page makeup. The computer must make it possible to move quickly from one program to another and to easily cut and paste portions from one document into another.

The vast majority of personal computers use the MS-DOS operating system, which is adequate for unillustrated documents, since typically only one program is required. For documents that interpose computer-generated graphics and scanned images with text, a more advanced foundation is necessary than the spartan features provided by DOS. What's needed is an "operating environment," a set of tools that makes it possible to work in a flexible manner with multiple programs.

The most obvious advantage of operating environments such as that provided by the Macintosh or by Microsoft Windows on IBM-compatible computers is the fact that you can open several windows on the screen and view the results of several programs at the same time. Less visible is the fact that the operating environment provides a standardized set of ground rules for the command structures used by software applications, making it possible for you to move back and forth between two programs without having to become accustomed to an entirely different mode of operation. For example, although various applications written for the Macintosh use different commands, the common mouse/pull-down menu/icon user interface makes it easy to learn and work with a new program. Another desirable feature of an operating environment, though not an essential one, is multitasking, which enables you to have more than one program running at the same time. Such a system lets you have two applications in view at the same time and makes it easy to cut and paste from one to another.

Advanced operating environments such as Microsoft Windows demand a more powerful computer system than the basic PC. They require large amounts of RAM, a hard disk, a graphics monitor, and a mouse. Another piece of equipment that plays a role in such a system is the scanner. As described in Chapter 8, the function of a scanner is to convert any sort of image into a matrix of pixel values suitable for processing by a computer. Scanners are particularly suitable for bringing line art (drawings and other sorts of pictures rendered in solid hues) into the system. The pictures can be cropped, scaled, and otherwise edited and manipulated either during scanning or later by a drawing program; they can then be merged with text in the page makeup program.

Merged text and graphics printing puts greater demands on the laser printer than text-only printing. Whereas for text-only applications a printer with a static page description language and a small amount of memory might suffice, the addition of graphics tends to require that the printer use a dynamic language, which provides the more complex graphics operations needed by the page makeup program. To accommodate memory-hungry graphics, the laser printer should have at least one megabyte of RAM, enabling a full page to be printed at 300 dpi.

Caveat Emptor

The computer market is not for the faint-hearted shopper. At best, the odds are somewhat less favorable than those of Russian roulette—especially with regard to purchases of software. For every program that turns out to be useful, probably one other is bought and then sits on a shelf because its functions were misunderstood, because it failed to function as claimed, because of unexpected hardware requirements, or because it was too difficult to use. In a new area such as desktop publishing, all the perennial problems are multiplied: bug-infested software, hastily written manuals, salespeople long on buzzwords but short on a basic understanding of the systems they're selling, a scarcity of organized user groups, and other problems are rife. If typography is a new realm for you, testing a program may not be a satisfactory way of determining its value. Any good program is going to look complicated, if only by virtue of the number of parameters that are involved in the publishing process. It's hard at first glance to see whether that complexity is the necessary result of the power of the program or simply a reflection of its awkwardness.

Where, then, can you get the kind of reliable information necessary to justify investing hundreds or thousands of dollars? By all means, don't accept at face value any general descriptions of products, especially buzzwords such as "WYSIWYG" or "near-typeset quality." Even if the salesperson sincerely believes these to be accurate descriptions, confusion over their actual meanings makes them useless or misleading. Nor is it satisfactory to shop on the basis of a list of features, since such a list conveys no sense of how easily any particular capability can be implemented. Magazine reviews (especially when negative) can provide some help, but are too often either unreliable, tainted by the prejudices of the author, or incomplete. Really useful guidance can only be had from other users of the system you are considering—and not just any users, but those who have applied the system to documents similar to yours. Don't buy a system until you have talked to such users. If you can't find any, ask the vendor for names of two or three.

As for prices, keep in mind that you are buying tools, and as with hand tools, there are light-duty, household models and heavy-duty, commercial-grade ones. Almost invariably, the extra expense of buying the right tool for the job is an investment well-made. On the other hand, don't make the mistake of thinking one program is better than another simply because it costs more. The desktop publishing market is simply too new and too uncharted for anyone to have a clear idea as to what the "right" price for a given level of functionality should be. Prices are all over the place.

A final major factor is how much value you place on your time. Desktop publishing programs now on the market boast many features, but implementing them can take more time than you are prepared to spend. A labor-intensive page makeup system may wind up being less cost-effective than making up pages using traditional pasteup. What may look easy and efficient in a software demonstration may eventually drive you crazy when you have to do it over and over again for file after file during the production process. If your needs for graphics are only occasional, you may be able to get by satisfactorily with a text-oriented system, pasting in your occasional graphic when necessary.

That advice—to resort to manual pasteup when necessary—is an appropriate conclusion for this book. No matter how powerful the advantages nor how hobbling the shortcomings of current desktop publishing systems may appear, it should always be remembered that these tools represent merely one set of options within a broad and constantly changing spectrum of methods. Like so many previous introductions to the field, personal computers and laser printers are rapidly merging into that spectrum, confirming that change—technical, procedural, and aesthetic innovation—is actually the oldest tradition of publishing.

How This Book Was Made

When we decided to produce this book using the same technologies we were writing about, there were many promising typesetting and pagination products on the horizon. As we go to press, most of them are still there. As you will find out when you shop for desktop publishing products, this is a field in which vendors speak of future products in the present tense.

We produced the manuscript text on a variety of IBM PC-compatible microcomputers—each of us using his favored word processing program—and saved the files as unformatted ASCII files prefatory to typesetting. Although we used spelling checkers, every word of the manuscript was reviewed by a copy editor before typesetting and by a proofreader afterwards.

The production tools we chose had to meet the high aesthetic demands of commercial book work, but most of the first generation of desktop publishing tools did not make the grade, especially in the area of typographic control. For our text formatting, we chose MagnaType—a commercial typesetting program from Magna Computer Systems—because of its excellent typographic capabilities. Although MagnaType currently lacks any on-screen page preview capability—a very useful tool—this shortcoming was outweighed by the precise control it gave us over the typesetting process. We ran MagnaType on an IBM PC AT with a 30 megabyte hard disk, which provided the speed and storage necessary for efficient production. Before importing the text into MagnaType, we did some preparatory coding in our word processors. This consisted mainly of inserting flags for subheads, paragraph endings, and chapter titles.

The version of MagnaType we used does not integrate graphics into pages, but using its companion program MagnaPage—a book pagination program—we

Epilogue

created complete text pages leaving windows (complete with border rules) for artwork that was added later with traditional paste-up methods. The pagination program automatically added crop marks, running heads, and folios. The text pages were proofed on an Apple LaserWriter Plus using MagnaType's typesetter emulation utilities and typeset on a Linotron 202N CRT digital typesetter manufactured by Linotype Corporation.

Most of the graphics in the book were created by the authors using Microsoft Word 1.05 and Aldus Corporation's PageMaker 1.2 running on an Apple Macintosh Plus. Although commercial typographic capabilities are slow coming to the Macintosh, it runs circles around the PC when it comes to highly interactive graphic work. These illustrations were proofed on a LaserWriter, then typeset using a PostScript-equipped Linotype Linotronic L100 laser typesetter driven by a Macintosh Plus.

The book's text is set in the Palatino and Helvetica families from the Mergenthaler typeface library. Most of the figure type is Times Roman with Palatino Italic from the Adobe Systems' collection of PostScript typefaces.

Glossary

artwork   Any nontext material, including photographs, drawings, graphs, charts, patterns, rules, boxes, and background tints.

ascender   The stroke of a lower case letter that extends above the body of the letter.

ASCII   American Standard Code for Information Interchange, a widely-adopted numbering scheme for characters and control commands: 0 to 32 is reserved for nonprinting control commands; 33 to 127 for standard keyboard characters. Codes from 128 to 256 are referred to as "high-bit ASCII," and the use of these characters varies among different systems.

baseline   The invisible line upon which the bottoms of typeset characters align.

batch pagination   The automated page makeup of whole manuscripts by a computer program acting on a set of preestablished criteria for placement of text and graphic elements.

bit maps   Computer-generated drawings composed of dots with each dot assigned to a specific location. Digital imaging systems work by creating bit maps of text and graphics and having the output device precisely reproduce the arrangements of dots on paper, photosensitive film, or other substrate.

blue line   A page proof created from film negatives just prior to printing. The same negatives are used to produce printing plates, hence the blue line is an accurate representation of the pages as they will be printed.

cap height   The height of the capital letters in a given typeface.

color separation   A photomechanical or electronic process of creating from a color photograph three or four film negatives representing the three primary colors (red, yellow, and blue) and possibly black. Each of these negatives is used to create a separate printing plate for each color. When the colors are overprinted, the color of the original photograph is faithfully reproduced.

column balancing   Evening the length of the columns on the final page of a chapter in a multiple-column layout.

Glossary

composition In typesetting, the process of assembling the typographic commands from the front-end computer into a set of commands that drive the typesetter.

condensed In typography, type whose character widths have been reduced while maintaining original cap height.

continuous tone image A graphic, such as a photograph, that includes intermediate gray levels.

decorative face A typeface whose design is strongly evocative, such as script and calligraphic faces.

descenders The parts of letters that extend below the baseline, as in the lower strokes of a *g* or *p*.

device independence The ability to print the same document on a variety of different output devices.

digital printer A typesetter of printer that creates character images by building them of many small dots.

digital type Type created from an electronic font whose character images are built up from minute dots created by the typesetter.

digitizer A device that samples the intensity of white in a continuous tone image and converts it into a grid of grayscale values.

dingbats Ornamental typographic elements used as page adornments, borders, and highlights.

display face Typefaces designed for use in large sizes, typically over 18 points. Their designs tend to be bold or eye-catching, and they are used commonly for signs and headlines.

dithering The use of computer-generated patterns to simulate shades of gray.

dot matrix A printing technology that uses a matrix of small pins as its impact mechanism.

driver A computer program that translates instructions from a front-end computer into a series of commands written in a form that can be interpreted by a printer or typesetter.

duotone A printed graphic image rendered in two colors, one of which is typically black.

dynamic page description language A page description language in which commands can be combined in a flexible manner to form new commands.

electro-erosion   A type of printer that uses polarized light to vaporize the coating of aluminized paper, creating dots of black.

electrophotographic   A class of printers that uses light sources such as lasers and light-emitting diodes to produce a pattern of electrical charges on a light-sensitive drum.

em   In typography, a unit of measure equal to the point size of the type in which it is used. When setting 14-point type, then, an em equals 14 points. An em space is a unit of horizontal distance, whose dimension is reckoned in this same way.

en   In typography, a unit of measure equal to half an em, or one half the size of the type in which it is used. An en space is half as wide as an em space.

escapement   Originally, the horizontal movement during typewriting after a letter was struck. The movement was sufficient to allow the striking of the next letter without overprinting or undue space between letters. In computer typesetting, escapement is an expression of the horizontal distances between imaged characters. Character widths are expression of escapement, and the escapement accorded specific letters is modified by kerning variations and adjustments to tracking.

expanded   In typography, type whose character widths have been increased while maintaining original cap height.

feathering   Adjusting the leading of a column of text to slightly increase its length.

fixed space   In typography, a unit of horizontal measurement (such as an em or en) that is not subject to compression or expansion during hyphenation and justification.

folios   Page numbers.

font   The matrix from which characters of a typeface are generated. Computerized fonts consist of electronic data that describe all aspects of the complete character set of a given typeface.

footer   A typographic element repeated at the bottom of successive pages, typically including folios.

four-color process   Printing using inks representing the four primary colors (red, yellow, and blue) from which all other printed colors are generated. A separate printing plate must be made for each color.

front end   The host computer that drives a typesetter.

Glossary

generic coding   A text labeling scheme in which all text elements are named according to a uniform standard. Text so labeled can be typeset on any system by creating a translation table that converts these generic labels into the specific typographic codes used by that system.

grayscale   The range of increments of intensity between pure black and pure white.

gutter   A vertical band of white, unprinted space that divides columns of type on a page or in a table.

halftone   A printable version of a graphic, typically a photograph, created by rendering the image as a pattern of dots. Continuous tones between solid color and white are achieved by varying the size and density of the dots.

header   A typographic element repeated at the tops of successive pages, typically containing chapter or manuscript titles and often folios.

high-bit ASCII   See ASCII.

h&j   See **hyphenation and justification**.

hyphenation and justification   The process of filling a measured line with type. As many letters as possible are set on the line, and hyphenation of words is a device for achieving this end. Space not taken up by the letters themselves is distributed throughout the line between letters and/or words (in justified type) or at the ends of the lines (in ragged type).

ink jet   A non-impact dot matrix printer that applies ink directly to paper through tiny jet nozzles.

italic   A slanted variation of a typeface, whose design is often derived from calligraphic forms (see **oblique**).

justified type   Type set in columns whose left and right margins are vertically straight. Extra space on a line is distributed between letters and or words to force the line of type to completely fill the measure.

kerning   The process of adjusting the spaces between letters on a case-by-case basis to accommodate the varying shapes of letters and how those shapes interact. The goal of kerning is to achieve even, consistent letter spacing without distracting gaps or crowding.

laser printer   A type of printer that uses a spinning mirror to scan the modulated beam of a stationary laser across a light-sensitive drum, producing a pattern of electrical charges that attract toner particles, which are offset onto paper.

leading   The vertical distance between lines of type, measured in points and fractions of points.

line art   Graphics that can be represented in one solid color with no intermediate color levels between solid inking and white.

logical hyphen   A hyphen added to type during hyphenation and justification whose placement has been determined by the computer through the application of a series of grammatical rules, not through the use of dictionary.

macros   Groups of operations that can be invoked with a single command.

magnetography   A raster printing technique in which a charge is created on a print drum using writing heads similar to those used in disk drives.

measure   In typography, the maximum allowable length to which a line of type may be set.

mechanical   The master image of a page from which reproductions are made. In traditional processes, the mechanical contains text and graphic elements pasted in place and ready for photographic reproduction.

monospaced type   Type in which all characters of a given typeface are accorded the same width, as on a typewriter.

multitasking   The running of two computer programs concurrently.

numeral space   In typography, a horizontal space equal in width to the numerals of a given typeface. It is used as an aid in aligning numbers in tabular material, such as financial reports.

object graphics   Images stored by a computer system in the form of mathematical descriptions of their components, making then independent of any single output resolution.

oblique   In typography, a slanted complement to a roman typeface created by inclining the letters to the right. The letters themselves by and large maintain their original forms except for this slant. Some typefaces are designed as obliques, others are the result of the front-end computer's distortion of a roman face (**see italic**).

offset lithography   A printing technique based on the immissibilty of water and oil-based inks. Printing plates are photographically created from film negatives of pages, and printing areas take on a surface quality that allows ink to adhere. The rest of the plate is wetted, so it repels the ink. The inked image is offset onto an intermediate surface from which the paper itself is printed.

old-style numbers   Numerals of some typefaces that don't sit on the baseline.

opaquing   The process of eliminating small flaws in photographic images of pages prior to the creation of the printing plates. The flaws are usually small specks that appear on the film and will print as such unless they are painted over.

orphan   The opening line of a paragraph isolated at the bottom of a column.

outline fonts   Computerized fonts which create character images based on a set of master outlines stored in electronic form. When a specific point size is called for, the computer scales the outline to the appropriate size and sends it to the typesetter with instructions for filling it in with black.

pair kerning   The adjustment of the spaces between specific letter pairs by referring to a table containing the values of all such adjustments (see **sector kerning**).

page description language   A computer programming language whose vocabulary can express the description and placement of text and graphic elements on a page. The most complete page description language is one that can describe any page and any manipulation of text and graphics that can be achieved through traditional methods.

page grid   A structure that provides alignment guides for all text and graphic elements on a page or series of pages. Abiding by the grid speeds the page makeup process and assures design consistency from page to page.

pagination   The process of creating finished pages by means of a computer program, thus bypassing hand paste-up.

parallel communications   A data transmission technique in which data is sent over multiple side-by-side channels; generally faster than serial communications.

pasteup   The process of assembling pages through the hand pasting of text and graphic elements onto a sheet of paper or cardboard.

perfect binding   A binding process in which individual sheets or larger sheets folded into booklets are assembled in proper page order, glued at one edge, and wrapped with a cover. The glue holds the pages to each other and to the cover. After binding, the three open edges of book or magazine are evenly trimmed.

photostat   A photographic reproduction of line art.

phototypesetting   The process typesetting using photosensitive paper or film as an imaging substrate. Areas exposed to light inside the typesetter become black when run through a photographic developer process. The light sources within the typesetter include lasers and cathode ray tubes.

pica   A unit of measurement equal to .99624 inches and composed of 12 points.
pi font   A font of utility characters, such as mathematical or commercial symbols.

pixel   The smallest unit that can be displayed on a computer monitor or detected by a digitizer.

point   A unit of typographic measurement equal to one twelfth of a pica, or .166040 inches.

point size   An expression of letter size in typography, equal to slightly more than the distance from the top top a typeface's ascenders to the bottoms of its descenders.

pre-press   The stages of the preparation of printed matter prior to the printing stage. These include editorial, typesetting, design, and mechanical preparation.

primitives   Simple, general operations built into a hardware or software system that serve as building blocks for more complex commands.

printer buffer   A block of random-access memory, often contained in a separately cabled box, that provides a temporary storage area for files that are being transmitted to the printer.

printer controller   The computer built into a printer that processes data received from an external computer and drives the printer's imaging mechanism.

printer protocols   Sets of text formatting commands recognized by printers; refers generally to the simple sets of commands provided by popular dot matrix and daisy-wheel printers.

proportionally spaced type   Type in which letters have unique character widths as demanded by their individual designs (see **monospaced type**).

quads   In typography, non-printing spaces used to fill out a line of type.

ragged left   A style of setting type in which the hyphenation and justification program sets as many letters as possible on a line and then places all the remaining space at the left end of that line. This creates columns with a vertically straight right margin but with lines that do not all fill the column measure, giving the left margin an irregular, ragged appearance.

ragged right   A style of setting type in which the left margin is vertically straight, and all extra space on a line is placed at the right-hand end of the line, creating a ragged right margin (see **ragged left**).

RAM   Random access memory or dynamic memory, erased when the power source is turned off.

RAM-resident utilities   Small programs that are loaded into the dynamic memory of a computer to add special functions to an application.

randomizing   A technique of rendering shades of gray by varying the density of printed dots.

raster graphics   Images stored by a computer system in the form of a dot-by-dot representation; same as bit-mapped graphics.

raster image processor   A device that takes instructions from the front-end computer and creates bit maps that are imaged by the typesetter. Raster image processors typically use a page description language as a means of expressing the descriptions of these bit maps.

raster imaging   A method of type- and imagesetting that builds the images from tiny dots. Typically, the arrangements of these dots—called a bit map—is created by a raster image processor.

resolution   In digital imaging, a measure of the number of dots per inch a typesetter can generate. This higher the resolution, the clearer are the final images, because the individual dots become to small to be detected by the eye. The resolution of commercial typesetters is typically over 1,000 dots per inch.

RIP   See **raster image processor**.

rippling   Automatic repagination of a document by a batch pagination program following an insertion or a deletion.

ROM   Read only or permanent memory, used for storing programs, fonts, and other basic data used by computers and printers.

roman   Typefaces designed with the standard upright characters typical of most Western text.

saddle stitching   A form of binding in which pages are assembled into one large booklet, and staples are driven through the center fold. The other three sides are then evenly trimmed.

sans serif   Typefaces that lack serifs, the small counter strokes at the ends of a letter's main strokes. San serif typefaces typically are made of strokes almost even in thickness throughout.

scanner   Same as digitizer.

screened art   Graphics that have been halftoned or which are created from a series of dots large enough to be reproduced by the printing press.

sector kerning   The process of adjusting the spaces between letters carried out by the computer based on calculations based on the shapes of adjoining letters. Kerning values are assigned by the program based on decisions about how adjoining shapes should best be spaced.

serial communications   A data transmission technique in which data is sent along a single channel, one bit a time; generally a slower process than parallel communications.

serifs   Short counter strokes at the ends of a letter's main strokes. Serifs aid the eye in sorting out the many strokes in a typeset passage and are an aid to a typeface's legibility.

sheet-fed press   A printing press that prints on pre-cut sheets of paper.

sidebar   In editorial and page design, a story within a story, often a sidelight or amplification of a point within the main text. Sidebars are typically designed to stand apart from the rest of the page.

small capitals   Capital letters that are smaller than a typeface's normal upper case character set. Small caps are used when words or passages of text need to be set in all caps and the use of full-size capitals would be visually disruptive.

solid leading   Line spacing in typography which the leading between lines is equal to the point size of the type being used, e.g. 10-point type set on 10 points of lead.

spaceband   The typographer's term for a word space.

static page description language   A page description language in which commands cannot be combined to form new commands.

stripping   The assembly of all of the photographic negatives necessary to create printing plates, including all halftones and color separation, all in precise registration.

style sheet   A reference guide used by some text processors that contains all of the typographic specifications for a particular text element. This element is given a label, and when the text processor finds this label, it refers to the style sheet for the parameters associated with it (see **generic coding**).

supermicro   A computer that uses advanced microcomputer technology to achieve performance levels previously associated with minicomputers.

symbol set   The collection of symbols used in a font.

text face   A typeface designed for maximum legibility, readability, and beauty at text sizes, typically from 10 to 12 point.

tombstoning   In page design, the stacking of similarly shaped text or graphic elements that gives the page a blocky, segmented appearance.

Glossary

tracking The overall letterspacing in a passage of text. Tracking is typically tightened to counter the tendency of type to look too loosely set as point size increases.

typeface A set of characters, numerals, punctuation marks, and related symbols that have been designed with a consistent appearance.

typeface family A group of typefaces that share a common design approach, but which vary in stroke weight and character width. Type families typically include italic or oblique complements to the upright roman faces.

vertical justification Adjustments in leading to make a block of text fit within top and bottom margins.

web press A printing press that uses paper that is continually fed from one or a series of large rolls, as in a newspaper press.

white space In typography, the space between letters and words. In page design, the space between text and/or graphic elements on a page.

widow The final line of a paragraph isolated at the top of a column.

WYSIWYG An acronym for "what you see is what you get," referring to typographic and graphic design systems that represent on the computer's screen an image of what the final page will actually look like.

xerography An electrostatic printing and duplicating process based on the use of dry inks (toners) which are attracted to a surface upon which an image has been created by selectively charging certain areas electrostatically, usually using light to trigger the charging process. The toner pattern is then offset onto paper, where it is fused into place with heat.

x-height In typography, the height of the lower case letters, as typified by the height of the letter x.

Bibliography

Typographics and Design

Josef Muller-Brockmann, *Grid Systems in Graphic Design*, New York: Hastings House, 1986

Armin Hoffman, *Graphic Design Manual*, New York: Van Nostrand Reinhold, 1965

Philip B. Meggs, *A History of Graphic Design*, New York: Van Nostrand Reinhold, 1983

Pocket Pal, New York: International Paper Company, 1983

Ben Rosen, *Type and Typography*, New York: Van Nostrand Reinhold, 1976

James Craig, *Phototypesetting*, New York: Watson-Guptill, 1978

John Seybold, *Digital Typesetting*, Media, Pennsylvania: Seybold Publications, 1985

Hardware

Inside LaserWriter, Cupertino, California: Apple Computer Inc., 1986

James Cavuoto, *Laser Print It!*, Reading, Massachusetts: Addison-Wesley Publishing Company, 1986

Ted Nace and Michael Gardner, *LaserJet Unlimited*, Berkeley: Peachpit Press, 1986

Page Description Languages

Adobe Systems, Inc., *PostScript Language Reference Manual*, Reading, Massachusetts: Addison-Wesley Publishing Company, 1985

Bibliography

Adobe Systems, Inc., *PostScript Language Tutorial and Cookbook,* Reading, Massachusetts: Addison-Wesley Publishing Company, 1985

Graphics

Gregory R. Glau, *Business Graphics with the IBM PC/XT/AT,* Homewood, Illinois: Dow Jones-Irwin, 1986

Steve Lambert, *Presentation Graphics on the IBM PC,* Bellevue, Washington: Microsoft Press, 1986

Jerry Mar, *MacGraphics for Business,* Glenview, Illinois: Scott, Foresman and Company, 1986

Index

Index

Index

Index

180